UP FROM SLAVERY

CBSE Class XI

English-Hindi

ARIHANT PRAKASHAN, MEERUT

ARIHANT PRAKASHAN, MEERUT

卐 Administrative & Production Offices

Corporate Office 4577/15, Agarwal Road, Darya Ganj, New Delhi -110002
Tele: 011- 47630600, 23280316; Fax: 011- 23280316

Head Office Kalindi, TP Nagar, Meerut (UP) - 250002
Tele: 0121-2401479; Fax: 0121-2401648

卐 Sales & Support Offices

Agra, Ahmedabad, Bengaluru, Bhubaneswar, Chennai, Delhi(I&II), Guwahati, Haldwani, Hyderabad, Jaipur, Kolkata, Kota, Lucknow, Nagpur, Meerut, Patna & Pune

卐 ISBN 978-93-5176-528-8

Typeset by Arihant DTP Unit at Meerut

For further information about the products from Arihant, log on to www.arihantbooks.com or email to info@arihantbooks.com

Preface

The CBSE, in order to inculcate the habit of reading the descriptive work in students, has introduced this novel in the curriculum of class XI English Core. This book is prescribed keeping in view the flair of the text and simplicity of the plot of the novel so that the student can acknowledge easily while reading it.

"Up from Slavery" by Booker. T. Washington is a real-life experience, during the time of Civil War. It begins with recollection of the author's birth and follows his progress through his education and establishment of Tuskegee Institute.

This series has been specially prepared with the purpose to make the reading of novels easy and less time consuming. The novel has been covered in English & Hindi Language both because reading in English is takes more time than in Hindi. For this reason, we have tried to make the reading easy by giving the material in both Hindi & English Language, so that the students can understand the content of the novels in a comfortable way and then write the perfect answers.

We have tried to help out the students in all aspects to learn this novel in such a way so that they will become competent enough to answer the questions that will come in exams. We hope the students will relish this book.

Novel Outline

About the Novel

The protagonist of the book is **Booker T. Washington** himself who spends his life trying to raise his people up from slavery. He very patiently works on every venture and finally founds the Tuskegee Institute in order to promote education. The Antagonists include the white people who have to be won over and whom Booker believes to be decent and good and his own race whose faith he has to keep alive.

The end of the book comes with his address to the Atlanta Exposition, where it is the first time that a Negro stands on the same platform as the whites. Here he uses the metaphor of "Cast your buckets down" and is congratulated for uplifting his people. At the end of his autobiography in 1901, Booker found optimism for his race in America. That feeling came because of his speech in Richmond, Virginia, in a building where he had slept once under a wooden side walk.

The autobiography begins with Booker's recollection of his birth in Virginia and carries on with his progress through his education, the Tuskegee Institute and his popularity as a speaker presenting the importance of good race relations to many audiences. The most important theme is that of the value of education.

Throughout the novel he emphasizes on this since he had been denied the right to learn and once he was free he wanted to soak up learning. The next important theme is that of dignity of work. According to Booker, no education is complete, without learning a trade. He felt that his race could never rise up without earning a trade.

Slavery is often presented thematically. Booker believed that slavery affected the Negroes but morally it affected the whites also, so no one could escape the terrible impact of slavery. The relationship between the races is another theme. Booker came to understand that he had the influence to reach as many people of both the races to convince them that a good relationship between them was very valuable for the growth of the individual, community and nation.

The last of the themes involves the idea that success is measured by the obstacles we have to overcomes to reach our goal. Booker felt that a man's character was built by how many walls he had to climb over before he reached his destination.

The process of achievement was more important than the finished product. The overall mood is one of optimism where he believes that whites and blacks living together is not only possible but very much probable.

Novel के बारे में...

इस पुस्तक के नायक **बुकर टी. वाशिंगटन** हैं जिन्होंने अपनी पूरी जिंदगी अपने लोगों को दासत्व से मुक्त करने में लगा दी, हर उद्यम पर बड़ी बारीकी से कार्य करके अंततः शिक्षा को प्रोत्साहित करने के लिए टस्कीज इंस्टीट्यूट को खोज निकाला। गोरे लोग प्रतिद्वंद्वी थे और उन पर विजय पाना, जिसे वे अच्छे व सभ्य समझते थे, और अपनी कौम के लोगों का भरोसा भी जीवित रखना था। इस पुस्तक का अंत Atlanta Exposition (अटलांटा प्रदर्शन) से हुआ जहाँ पर पहली बार एक नीग्रो तथा एक गोरा व्यक्ति एक साथ एक ही जगह खड़े हुए थे। यहाँ पर उन्होंने एक उपमा का प्रयोग किया था Cast your buckets down तथा उन्हें इसी जगह पर अपने लोगों के उत्थान के लिए बधाई दी गई थी। अपनी आत्मकथा के अंत में, 1901 में बुकर को आशा की किरण दिखाई दी थी कि उनकी प्रजाति भी अमेरिका में अब स्थान पा सकेगी। उनके मन में यह विचार इस वजह से आया था कि एक बार वह रिचमंड, वर्जिनिया के जिस भवन में लकड़ी के तख्ते के नीचे सोए थे आज इसी भवन में वे भाषण दे रहे थे।

आत्मकथा की शुरूआत बुकर के अपने जन्म, जो वर्जिनिया में हुआ था, से शुरू हुई थी। इसकी अगली कड़ी उनकी शिक्षा तथा टस्कीज इंस्टीट्यूट से जुड़ी है। बाद में उनकी एक वक्ता के तौर पर प्रसिद्धि तथा अलग-अलग कौम के आपसी रिश्तों के लिए कार्य को जाना गया। सबसे महत्त्वपूर्ण बिंदु था– शिक्षा की महत्ता। पूरे जीवनकाल में वे शिक्षा पर जोर देते रहे और इसकी महत्ता को वह भली-भाँति समझते थे, क्यों कि बचपन में उन्हें शिक्षा से वंचित कर दिया गया था और जब वे बड़े हो गए तो उन्हें इसकी जरूरत महसूस हुई। दूसरी जरूरी चीज थी–काम की गरिमा। बुकर के अनुसार कोई भी शिक्षा पूरी नहीं हो सकती जब तक उसके साथ कोई पेशा न हो। वे मानते थे कि उनकी कौम कभी भी उदय नहीं कर सकती है अगर उसमें कोई पेशा न जोड़ा जाए।

गुलामी कई बार विषय-वस्तु की दृष्टि से प्रस्तुत की जाती है। बुकर मानते थे कि दासत्व से नीग्रो तो प्रभावित हुए हैं पर गोरे लोग भी मानसिक रूप से प्रभावित हुए हैं। इसलिए दासत्व के प्रभाव से कोई भी बच नहीं सकता। अगली महत्त्वपूर्ण बात थी –कौम के बीच के आपसी रिश्ते। बुकर यह जानते थे कि उनके अंदर यह प्रभाव है कि वह दोनों कौम के लोगों के बीच जा सकते थे और उन्हें समझा सकते थे कि आपसी समन्वय से व्यक्तिगत व सामाजिक विकास संभव था।

अंतिम महत्त्वपूर्ण तथ्य था सफलता का मूल्यांकन इस बात से होना चाहिए कि अपने लक्ष्य प्राप्ति में कितनी बाधाओं को पार किया गया है। बुकर महसूस करते थे कि मनुष्य का चरित्र इस बात से तय होता है कि अपने लक्ष्य तक जाने में उसने कितनी दीवारें पार की हैं? समाप्ति से ज्यादा महत्त्वपूर्ण होता है –प्राप्त करने का तरीका। सबसे अच्छा आशावादी नजरिया यह होता है कि गोरे और काले एक साथ रह सकें जोकि संभव भी था और संभावित भी।

Know the Characters...

Booker T. Washington

This man's magic shines throughout his autobiography. In fact, he was very modest about his accomplishments. His life was amazing, because he took himself out of slavery and was full of determination to pull his people up with him. He took every opportunity to propose his ideas and philosophies to all races so that attitudes could change in America.

He saw that many terrible things were happening to his people, but still he remained quite optimistic that, with the help of education and hard work, they could effectively integrate with the dominant white society. He became famous because of his good works but never sought it out. He devoted his life to his students as well as his race and was sure that the day was not far when the black man would be totally accepted throughout the country.

Mrs. Ruffner

Mrs. Ruffner was the wife of owner of the salt mine where Booker worked in Maiden, West Virginia. She was a strict boss and many had quit the job or had been fired. Booker learnt that to make her happy, one had to understand that she wanted things clean, done promptly and systematically and wanted honesty and frankness.

Miss Mary F. Mackie

Miss Mary F. Mackie was the first person whom Booker met when he arrived at Hampton. On reaching there he was awestruck by the beauty of the school building and believed his life to have a new meaning. He could not make a favourable impression on the head teacher, Miss Mackie, since he was shabbily dressed.

Novel में उपस्थित प्रमुख व्यक्ति

बुकर टी. वाशिंगटन

उपन्यास का सर्वाधिक प्रधान चरित्र जिसका महत्त्व संपूर्ण उपन्यास में परिलक्षित होता है। Booker T Washington (बुकर टी. वाशिंगटन) एक महान् व्यक्ति थे, जो अपनी महान उपलब्धियों के बावजूद अत्यंत विनम्र थे। उनका जीवन आश्चर्यों से भरा हुआ था, क्योंकि उन्होंने स्वयं को दासता के अँधेरे से मुक्त कराया तथा अपनी जाति के लोगों की भलाई हेतु कार्य किया। उन्होंने America (अमेरिका) में सभी जाति के लोगों को अपने विचार समझाए एवं लोगों के नजरिये को बदलने का प्रयास किया।

उन्होंने देखा कि उनकी जाति के लोगों के साथ बहुत बुरा बर्ताव हो रहा था, परंतु वे आशावादी थे एवं उन्होंने उम्मीद जारी रखी कि परिश्रम एवं शिक्षा के बल पर उनकी जाति के लोग भी श्वेत समुदाय की बराबरी करने में सफल होंगे। वे अपने महान् कार्यों की वजह से विख्यात हो गए। उन्होंने अपना संपूर्ण जीवन अपने विद्यार्थियों के हित में तथा अपनी जाति के उत्थान में अर्पित कर दिया, क्योंकि उन्हें पूर्ण विश्वास था कि एक दिन ऐसा अवश्य आएगा जब Negro (नीग्रो) जाति के लोग पूर्ण विश्व में स्वीकार किए जाएँगे।

श्रीमती रफनर

Mrs Ruffner (श्रीमती रफनर) उस नमक की खान के स्वामी की पत्नी थीं, जिस खान में बुकर ने कार्य किया था एवं जो West Virginia (दक्षिण वर्जीनिया) में स्थित थी। वे एक कड़क मिजाज स्वामिनी थीं तथा इस कारण से उनके लिए काम करने वाले नौकरों को काम छोड़ देना पड़ता था अथवा वे उन्हें पदच्युत कर दिया करती थीं। बुकर ने यह अनुभव किया कि श्रीमती रफनर को प्रसन्न करने हेतु यह समझना आवश्यक था कि वे कार्यों को पूर्ण स्वच्छता के साथ, शीघ्रतापूर्वक तथा व्यवस्थित ढंग से किया जाना पसंद करती थीं

मैरी एफ. मैकी

मैरी एफ. मैकी प्रथम महिला थीं, जिनसे बुकर हैंपटन पहुँचने के पश्चात् सर्वप्रथम मिले। हैंपटन पहुँचने के पश्चात् उनकी आँखें आश्चर्य से विस्मित हो गईं, जब उन्होंने वहाँ विद्यालय का भवन देखा तथा उन्हें प्रशंसापूर्वक भवन को देखते रहने की इच्छा हुई, इस अनुभव ने उनकी जिंदगी को एक नया उद्देश्य दिया। वे मैरी एफ. मैकी पर अच्छा प्रभाव नहीं छोड़ सके, क्योंकि उन्होंने अत्यंत गंदे वस्त्र पहन रखे थे।

Up From Slavery

1

A Slave Among Slaves

Heritage of Booker T Washington

Booker remembers that he was born in a slave family on a plantation in Franklin County Virginia somewhere near a cross roads post office called, Hale's ford in 1858 or 1859. We used to live in a slave quarters, a typical log cabin about 14 by 16 square feet having my mother, a brother, a sister and myself, but was not sure of the year and place.

Phase of Revolution Against the Slavery

I had no schooling while I was a slave. The picture of several boys and girls in a school room had a deep impression on me and I felt that to study in this way would be the same as getting into paradise. The first time, I had the knowledge of the fact that we were slaves, when one early morning my mother was praying for the victory of Lincoln and his army.

Declaration of Freedom and Situation Afterwards

The slaves were all called to the Big House where they were told by the masters by the reading of Emancipation Proclamation that they were really free. But then, there was a change in feelings. For so many years, they had been slaves and now, there was a great cognition of being free.

Word Meaning

Miserable	– दयनीय	Desolate	– अकेलेपन की स्थिति
Ancestor	– पूर्वज	Mansion	– हवेली
Engraved	– भली-भाँति अंकित होना	Procured	– प्राप्त
Emancipation	– स्वतंत्रता	Flogging	– कोड़े मारना
Drift	– सामान्य भाव	Deprivation	– कमी

1

A Slave Among Slaves

बुकर टी वाशिंगटन की विरासत

Booker (बुकर) को याद है कि उनका जन्म 1858 या 1859 में Hale's Ford (हेल फोर्ड) नामक डाकघर के आस-पास, Franklin County Virginia (फ्रैंकलिन काउंटी वर्जिनिया) के बगानों में एक दास परिवार में हुआ था। हम दासों के लिए बने कमरों का प्रयोग करते थे, जोकि 14/16 वर्ग फुट का लकड़ी से बना एक चौकोर कमरा होता था, जिसमें मैं, मेरी माँ, भाई और बहन रहते थे, परंतु उन्हें अपने जन्म का वर्ष अथवा स्थान कुछ भी निश्चित रूप से याद नहीं था।

गुलामी के विरुद्ध संघर्ष का दौर

जब तक मैं दासता गें था, मैं कभी स्कूल नहीं गया। कक्षा में लड़के-लड़कियों का बैठकर पढ़ने की छवि ने मेरे मन पर गहरा प्रभाव डाला और मुझे ऐसा महसूस होता था कि स्कूल जाना स्वर्ग जाने के बराबर होता है। पहली बार, इस तथ्य का ज्ञान कि हम दास हैं मुझे तब हुआ जब एक सुबह मेरी माँ Lincoln (लिंकन) और उनकी सेना की विजय की दुआ कर रही थी।

मुक्ति की घोषणा एवं उसके बाद की स्थिति

सभी गुलामों को Big House (बिग हाउस) पर बुलाया गया, जहाँ उन्हें उनके मालिकों द्वारा मुक्ति घोषणा-पत्र को पढ़कर उनके मुक्त होने की सूचना दी गई, परंतु फिर विचारों में बदलाव आया। इतने वर्षों से वे सभी दास थे और अब उनके भीतर आजाद होने की भावना एक बड़ी अनुभूति थी।

Endure	– सहन करना	Burr	– अत्यंत खुरदरी सतह
Sham	– नकली	Tenderness	– सज्जनता
Gewgaws	– अल्प महत्ता वाली वस्तुएँ	Fidelity	– विश्वसनीयता
Treacherous	– धूर्त	Bowel	– शरीर का एक अंग
Oppressor	– तानाशाह	Stagnating	– रुका हुआ

Important Questions

Questions based on the Plot of the Chapter

Q 1. What did Booker know about his birth and childhood?

बुकर अपने जन्म तथा बचपन के विषय में क्या जानते थे?

बुकर को अपने जन्म स्थान का ज्ञात न होना – 1858 या 1859 में हेल फोर्ड नामक डाकघर के आस-पास होना – 14/16 वर्ग फुट का लकड़ी से बने चौकोर कमरे का होना – बुकर के परिवार की स्थिति अत्यंत दु:खद व दयनीय होना – बुकर का कठिन परिस्थितियों का सामना करना।

Ans. Booker knew that he was born in Virginia state, but he did not remember the exact place or exact date of his birth. He could be able to learn that he was born near a cross roads post office named Hale's Ford and the year was 1858 or 1859. He was not even aware of month of his birth. He knew only that a log cabin of 14 by 16 feet square was his birth place. His childhood living was quite miserable. Booker was not much aware of his childhood and birth, because he was born in a slave family. In those days, slaves were treated very unfairly in the society. In addition to this, the family members of Booker were also in miserable condition because Booker's family was facing the scarcity of resources. Booker always tried to fight with difficulties of his life in order to get better positions for himself. In later days of his life, Booker realised that for achieving something only determination is required.

Q 2. How did Booker come to know about slavery when he was a child?

बुकर जब बच्चे थे, तब उन्हें गुलामी के विषय में कैसे पता चला?

बुकर का प्रात: उठना – माता की प्रार्थना सुनकर उठना – अभियान की सफलता की प्रार्थना – लिंकन के नस्लभेद उन्मूलन अभियान की सफलता की कामना – गुलामों का सचेत होना – गुलामों में आजादी की इच्छा का जागना – लिंकन का मानवतावादी होना।

Ans. One early morning, Booker was awakened by his mother, who was praying about Lincoln's army and its successfulness for freedom then, he came to know about the bitter experience of slavery. That was an Era when revolution began to take place, slaves became aware of their rights and they started to protest against slavery.

Booker was not aware of the condition of his race in initial phase because he was not enough wise to understand the complex issues like slavery.

He came to know about slavery when he saw his mother first time praying for success of mission of great leader Abraham Lincoln. Leader Lincoln was a humanitarian person and he was also against of any type of discrimination in races.

In fact, it was the time when he started to take care of such serious social issues and then Booker started framing plans regarding betterment of his race.

Q 3. How did the slaves react to the Emancipation Proclamation?

मुक्ति घोषणा-पत्र पर गुलामों की क्या प्रतिक्रिया थी?

मुक्ति घोषणा-पत्र का अत्यंत बेसब्री से गुलामों द्वारा प्रतीक्षा करना – प्रसन्नता एवं हर्षोल्लास – लंबी अवधि की दासता से मुक्ति तथा आनंद।

Ans. The Emancipation Proclamation brought an immense pleasure feeling for all slaves. All were filled with excitement and expectancy before that momentous morning.

All slaves were very happy, they had a feeling of deep interest, but there were no bitterness towards their old cruel masters. The slaves were told that they all were free which gave them tears of joy. In fact, slaves were very much eager about getting freedom because they were feeling very hopeless because of slavery.

They were loyal towards their masters, but they wanted to get freedom of living their lives according to their views. The white masters were very cruel towards their slaves which was also a factor that continuously induced them to get freedom.

2

Boyhood Days

Post Freedom Era for Slaves

The coming of freedom convinced the Negroes that they need to change their names and to leave the plantation for at least a few days to try out their freedom. My father, who was found his way into the new state of West Virginia.

Booker's Eagerness for Getting Educated

Booker's first step to education was his recognising the number 18 which was the barrel number of his step father at salt mine, where he worked. This made him attracted to learning and an intense longing for education grew in him. His mother got him a 'blue black' spelling book, which contained alphabet. He quickly finished that book.

Booker was not Allowed to Quit Work

Booker was disappointed as his step-father could not afford to allow him to quit working and to attend the school with other childern. So, his mother arranged with the teacher to give Booker lessons at night. He finally succeeded in his desire as long as he went to work in the furnace till - 9 o'clock, go to school and after the school would immediately come to work.

Some Problems Faced by Booker

The first problem faced by Booker was getting a cap or hat because the other children wore hats or caps on their heads, and he had neither hat nor cap. Booker told that we did not have money to buy or store a hat, my mother got two pieces of homespun and sewed them together, and I was soon the proud possessor of my first cap.

2

Boyhood Days

गुलामों के लिए आजादी के बाद का समय

आजाद होने के बाद Negroes (नीग्रो) व्यक्तियों ने अपना नाम बदलने तथा बगीचों से कुछ दिनों के लिए दूर जाने का निर्णय लिया, जिससे वे अनुभव कर सकें कि वे वास्तव में आजाद हैं। मेरे पिता को West Virginia (पश्चिम वर्जिनिया) नामक एक राज्य में नौकरी मिल गई थी।

शिक्षित होने के लिए बुकर की उत्सुकता

नमक की खान में उनके सौतेले पिता को 18 संख्या वाला बैरक मिला, जिसे देखकर बुकर ने संख्याओं को पहचानने की प्रक्रिया द्वारा पहली बार शिक्षित होने की उत्सुकता दिखाई। यहीं से वह सीखने की ओर आकर्षित हुए तथा उनके मन में शिक्षित होने की तीव्र लालसा जागने लगी। उनकी माता ने उनके लिए 'Blue Black' (ब्लू-ब्लैक) नामक अक्षरों की एक पुस्तक लाकर दी। उन्होंने यह पुस्तक शीघ्र ही पढ़ ली।

बुकर को काम छोड़ने की अनुमति नहीं थी

Booker (बुकर) के सौतेले पिता ने उन्हें काम छोड़कर अन्य बच्चों के साथ पढ़ाई करने की अनुमति नहीं दी, जिससे वे बहुत दुखी हो गए। अत: बुकर की माता ने उनके लिए घर पर ही एक शिक्षक का प्रबंध कर दिया, जो उन्हें रात्रि में पढ़ा सके। अंत में वह सफल हुए तथा 9 बजे तक भट्ठी में काम करने के बाद उन्हें विद्यालय जाने की अनुमति मिल गई, परंतु वहाँ से उन्हें वापस काम पर जाना होता था।

बुकर का कुछ समस्याओं से सामना

बुकर के सामने प्रथम समस्या एक हैट या टोपी प्राप्त करने की थी, क्योंकि अन्य बच्चे अपने सिरों पर हैट या टोपी पहना करते थे और उनके पास न तो हैट थी और न ही टोपी। बुकर ने बताया कि हमारे पास टोपी खरीदने के पैसे नहीं थे, मेरी माँ को घर में काते हुए कपड़े के दो टुकड़े मिले और उन्हें इकट्ठा सिलकर मैं गर्व के साथ अपनी पहली टोपी का धारक बन गया।

The Second Difficulty was with Regard to Booker's Name

When Booker joined the school, he noticed that almost every student had long name containging atleast two words. When the teacher asked Booker's name, he told his teacher that Booker Washington his name. Later, he came to know that he was given name Booker Taliaferro Washington by his mother. So, he decided to add this with his name and finally he became Booker T Washington.

उनका बुकर नाम होना अगली समस्या थी

जब बुकर ने स्कूल जाना प्रारंभ किया तो उन्होंने देखा कि लगभग सभी बच्चों के दो शब्दों से जुड़कर बने लंबे नाम हैं। शिक्षक ने जब बुकर से उसका नाम पूछा तो उन्होंने अपना नाम Booker Washington (बुकर वाशिंगटन) बताया। उन्हें बाद में पता चला की उनकी माता ने उनका नाम Booker Taliaferro Washington (बुकर टेलियाफेरो वाशिंगटन) रखा था। अत: उन्होंने इसे अपने नाम के साथ जोड़ने का निश्चय किया और अंतत: उनका नाम बुकर टी वाशिंगटन हो गया।

Word Meaning

Tedious	– कठिन	Occasion	– अवसर
Recognise	– पहचानना	Induce	– प्रेरित करना
Timid	– कायर	Disposition	– गुण
Perplexing	– भ्रमित करने वाली	Severe	– गंभीर रूप से
Temptation	– लालच	Possessor	– स्वामी, मालिक
Confrontation	– सामना	Penitentiary	– कारागार
Reliance	– विश्वास	Obstacles	– मार्ग में आने वाले अवरोध
Dreaded	– भयभीत	Aspirations	– उम्मीदें
Attainment	– उपलब्धि	Consolation	– सांत्वना

Important Questions

Questions based on the Plot of the Chapter

Q 1. What did Booker think about their first sign of freedom? How did he get his name as Booker T Washington?

बुकर ने आजादी की पहली निशानी के बारे में क्या सोचा? उनका नाम बुकर टी वाशिंगटन कैसे पड़ा?

गुलामी खत्म होने के बाद गुलामों ने मालिकों द्वारा दिए गए उपनामों को त्याग दिया – गुलाम ने खुद के लिए नया उपनाम चुना – बुकर के लिए सही मायनों में आजादी की शुरूआत थी – विद्यालय में सबके बड़े नाम थे – बुकर ने अपना नाम 'बुकर वाशिंगटन' बताया – माता द्वारा दिया गया 'टेलियाफेरो' नाम भी बुकर ने अपने नाम के मध्य में जोड़ लिया – आजादी के बाद बुकर की जिंदगी में बदलाव – स्कूल के समय में बुकर के नाम में परिवर्तन – बुकर टी वाशिंगटन नाम रखना।

Ans. When the slaves got freedom, they did not continue to bear the surname of their former owners and most of them took different surname, which was the first sign of freedom for Booker also. Later, when Booker joined school, he noticed that almost every student had long name containing atleast two words, so when the teacher asked his name, he told his teacher that Booker Washington was his name.

Later, he came to know that he was given name Booker Taliaferro by his mother. So, he decided to add this with his name and finally he became 'Booker T Washington'.

After getting freedom, many things changed in lives of slave. This was a pleasant and new experience for them. Booker also felt very relaxed, when he knew about emancipation announcement.

Slaves got a chance of their name editing after freedom because during slavery, slaves had to carry the surnames given by their masters which was quite disappointing for all slaves.

After getting freedom, maximum slaves either edited their surnames or changed their full names. Booker discovered his name himself during his school days where he told his teacher that his name was Booker T Washington.

Q 2. Describe two incidents that emphasise Booker's extreme love for education.

किन्हीं दो घटनाओं का उल्लेख कीजिए, जिनसे बुकर के अध्ययन के प्रति जागरूकता का पता चलता है?

पूरे परिवार के साथ दक्षिण वर्जिनिया प्रांत में आकर बसना – नमक की खान में काम करते समय संख्या 18, जो उनके सौतेले पिता की बैरक संख्या थी – उनकी माता ने उन्हें शब्दकोश एवं वर्णमाला की एक पुस्तक दी – उन्होंने कम समय में ही पूरी तरह पढ़ लिया – बुकर की माँ का साथ देना।

Ans. *Booker was very much eager about getting education, when we see following events we get proof of it*

(a) When he was a little boy, he came to west Virginia with family after freedom and he got employment in a salt mine. When he saw the number 18 there which was the number of barrel. he recognised that quickly and learnt that.

(b) When his mother gave him a book which contained spellings and alphabets, he finished the whole book very soon.

Actually Booker was very much interested in learning new things from his childhood days. His mother was aware of his this speciality so she always supported him and tried to provide him help as much as possible.

Booker started to learn elementary knowledge on his own behalf and for this he began to devote his idle time towards self-studies.

His plan was successful but he could not devote himself in studies completely as he was a slove boy, so he usually got least spare time to do any other work.

Q 3. Which two difficulties did Booker face when he found himself at the school for the first time? How did Booker find solutions to these problems?

बुकर को प्रथम बार विद्यालय में किन दो कठिनाइयों का सामना करना पड़ा? इन समस्याओं से निपटने हेतु बुकर ने क्या किया?

प्रथम बार विद्यालय में उन्हें दो कठिनाइयों का अनुभव हुआ – सभी छात्रों द्वारा टोपियाँ पहनना – बुकर की माँ द्वारा दो कपड़ों को सिलकर उनके लिए टोपी बनाकर परेशानी हल करना – नाम की समस्या उन्होंने स्वयं हल कर ली – आर्थिक स्थिति अच्छी न होना – बुकर के लिए टोपी का प्रबंध करना।

Ans. When Booker joined the school for first time, he faced two difficulties-all of the other students wore caps or hats which perplexed him and his name contained a single word where as others had long names.

He solved both of his problems in following way-

(a) He discussed hat related problem with his mother and his mother sewed two pieces of jeans to make a hat for him.

(b) He told the teacher that Booker Washington was his name which was a long name containing two words.

Booker was very wise and he had a positive approach for life related problems. He never lost his patience and this was the reason of his success in his all efforts.

Booker knew that his financial conditions was not much better to buy new things so he dicussed his problem with his mother, who was always prepared to solve his life related every issues.

Booker's mother never wanted to let him feel inferior in any situation so she arranged a cap for her son Booker. Booker discovered a full name for himself and when his teacher asked his name, he said that his name was 'Booker T Washington'. It was a name containing three words which was in fashion among students of those era.

3

The Struggle for an Education

Hampton Institute: Booker's Dream

One day while working in the coal-mine, Booker came to know about Hampton Institute at Virginia, meant particularly for the Negro people. In addition to that, the students would also be made familiar with some kind of trade or industry. Booker decided to reach there as early as he could.

Circumstances not Favourable for Booker

Booker was aware of his poor financial position and of the money he required to reach Hampton Institute. He took up a new job in the house of Mrs Ruffner who was known to be a strict disciplinarian. He very early gained trust of the lady and she encouraged Booker to read and learn. She also wanted him to head to Virginia for school education. His brother gave him all the money he could to help him achieve his dreams.

The Toughest Journey of Booker's Life

The distance from Malden to Hampton was about 500 miles. Booker did not have enough money to pay his journey. He had to go many days without food and slept on footpath. After travelling 82 miles from Hampton using different modes of transport, he reached Richmond. There, he noticed a ship unloading a of pig-iron. He worked long hours in the ship to earn money.

3

The Struggle for an Education

हैम्पटन इंस्टीट्यूट : बुकर का सपना

कोयले की खदान में काम करते हुए एक दिन Booker (बुकर) को Virginia (वर्जिनिया) के Hampton Institute (हैम्पटन इंस्टीट्यूट) के विषय में पता चला, जो केवल नीग्रो जाति के लोगों के लिए अत्यंत उत्तम विद्यालय था। छात्रों के लिए रोजगारपरक विषयों तथा उद्योगों के विषय में जानने के लिए भी पर्याप्त अवसर उपलब्ध थे। बुकर ने जल्द-से-जल्द वहाँ पहुँचने का निर्णय लिया।

बुकर के लिए परिस्थितियों का प्रतिकूल न होना

बुकर की आर्थिक स्थिति उन्हें अनुमति नहीं देती थी कि वह हैम्पटन इंस्ट्रीट्यूट जाए। उन्होंने Mrs Ruffner (श्रीमती रफनर) जोकि एक अत्यत अनुशासनप्रिय एवं कड़क मिजाज महिला थीं, के घर में काम करने का निर्णय लिया। उन्होंने जल्द ही उस महिला का विश्वास हासिल कर लिया और उन्होंने बुकर को पढ़ने एवं सीखते रहने के लिए प्रेरित किया। वह चाहती थी कि स्कूली शिक्षा के लिए वह वर्जिनिया जाए। उनके भाई ने भी अपनी जमा पूँजी उन्हें दे दी, जिससे वह अपने सपने को पूरा कर सके।

बुकर के जीवन की कठिनतम यात्रा

Malden (मालडेन) से हैम्पटन तक की दूरी लगभग 500 मील थी। बुकर के पास यात्रा के किराए हेतु पर्याप्त पैसे नहीं थे। उन्हें कई दिनों तक भूखा रहना पड़ा तथा फुटपाथ पर सोना पड़ा। कई प्रकार के साधनों का प्रयोग करते हुए उन्होंने हैम्पटन से 82 मील की यात्रा पूरी की तथा Richmond (रिचमंड) पहुँचे। वहाँ उन्होंने एक जहाज देखा, जिसमें से कच्चा लोहा उतारा जा रहा था। धन का प्रबंध करने हेतु उन्होंने कई घंटों तक उस जहाज पर काम किया।

Booker's Achievements

Booker was impressed to see General Samuel Armstrong, who helped the Negro schools at the close of the war by assisting in lifting up the Negro race. Many teachers helped Booker in getting clothes. Booker learnt etiquettes like table manners at Hampton. One thing that Booker learnt at Hampton that books could not teach was humanity and service to mankind, which General Armstrong was doing for the Negroes. Booker called it the most thrilling period of the American history.

बुकर की उपलब्धियाँ

बुकर Samuel Armstrong (सैमुअल आर्मस्ट्रांग) नामक शख्स से मुलाकात करने के बाद अत्यधिक प्रभावित हुए, जिसने युद्ध समाप्ति के बाद Negro (नीग्रो) जाति के उत्थान के लिए नीग्रो के विद्यालयों की सहायता की। बुकर के लिए बहुत से अध्यापकों ने वस्त्रों का प्रबंध किया। बुकर ने हैम्पटन में सभ्य समाज की रीतियाँ सीखी। एक चीज जो बुकर ने हैम्पटन में सीखी वह थी मानवता तथा सद्भावना, जो किताबी ज्ञान से ज्यादा महत्त्वपूर्ण है तथा जो जनरल आर्मस्ट्रांग नीग्रो जाति के लिए करते थे। बुकर के अनुसार यह American History (अमेरिकन इतिहास) की सबसे ज्यादा रोमांचकारी अवधि थी।

Word Meaning

Attractions – आकर्षण
Half Hearted – शंका के साथ
Exhaustion – थकावट
Fortune – सौभाग्य
Liberal – उदारवादी रवैया
Precious – मूल्यवान
Prevailing – सर्वव्याप्त
Part – अंश
Welcome – स्वागत
Acquaintance – मुलाकात
Regularly – नियमित रूप से
Devotional – आध्यात्मिक
Inspiring – प्रेरणादायी
Resolve – दृढ़ निश्चय करना
Bitterness – दुर्भावना
Cordial – मित्रतापूर्ण
Estimation – विचार
Revelation – सच का सामना करना
Earnest – निष्ठावान
Service – सेवा
Improve – सुधार
Generosity – उदारता
Prejudice – भेदभाव
Privilege – सम्मान
Pleasure – आनंद
Surprise – आश्चर्य

Important Questions

Questions based on the Plot of the Chapter

Q 1. How did Booker's experiences at Mrs Ruffner's house help him in getting admission in the Hampton Institute?

श्रीमती रफनर के घर कार्य करते हुए बुकर ने जो अनुभव प्राप्त किए उन अनुभवों ने उनकी हैम्पटन इंस्टीट्यूट में प्रवेश लेने हेतु किस प्रकार मदद की?

श्रीमती रफनर – एक अत्यंत कड़क मिजाज तथा अनुशासनप्रिय महिला थीं – वहाँ भी प्रधानाध्यापिका ने उन्हें कमरा साफ करने का काम दिया – अपने पुराने अनुभव के आधार पर उन्होंने मन लगाकर काम किया – सफाई से प्रभावित होकर प्रधानाध्यापिका ने उन्हें प्रवेश दे दिया।

Ans. Mrs Ruffner was very strict and disciplined in her approach. Her fastidious nature compelled Booker to do his job with complete dedication which became his habit in the later days and it helped him in getting admission in the Hampton Institute where he was given a work of room cleaning by headmistress of the institute. This task was a chance for Booker to prove his efficiency and capability in bearing responsibilities and because of his experience at Mrs Ruffner's house, he performed this task with full enthusiasm which finally became the cause of his admission in the Hampton Institute as the headmistress was very impressed by Booker's work.

When Booker joined his job at Mrs Ruffner's house, he found it difficult to please her because of her different nature. Mrs Ruffner was not wrong in her approach because she wanted everything in perfect order with maximum possible neatness. It was practically a little bit tough to perform every task according to her expectations every time, but Booker was very sincere and tried his best to satisfy her.

This became his habit in later days and he started doing everything with extreme care and perfection.This habit of Booker made him a successful person because he never took any work lightly in his whole life.

Q 2. Explain in brief how Booker reached Hampton Institute and got admission.

बुकर का हैम्पटन पहुँचने तथा हैम्पटन इंस्टीट्यूट में प्रवेश लेने की प्रक्रियाओं का संक्षेप में वर्णन कीजिए।

बुकर के लिए हैम्पटन इंस्टीट्यूट की यात्रा आसान न होना – कई साधनों का प्रयोग करते हुए उनका रिचमंड पहुँचना – जहाज पर काम करते हुए भावी खर्चों के लिए धन एकत्रित करना – हैम्पटन इंस्टीट्यूट पहुँचना – परीक्षा के रूप में प्रधानाध्यापिका द्वारा उन्हें कमरा साफ करने का काम देना।

Ans. Booker's journey to his dream institute was not easy. He did not have enough money so he started his journey with a lot of worries. Adopting various modes of conveyance, he reached Richmond where he worked on a ship and collected some amount for his further expenditures. He performed his task with full enthusiasm which made headmistress very satisfied and he got his admission in the Hampton Institute.

Booker was not ready to give up easily so he applied his best possible efforts in achieving his goal. He knew that reaching Hampton and getting admission there would not be a simple task so he was well prepared to face the challenges.

Booker was habitual to face adverse conditions so he did not become much concerned about possible difficulties. Instead of thinking about any other issue, he kept himself focused and continued his journey towards his goal. Finally, he succeeded in accomplishing his goal by overcoming challenges.

Questions based on the Character-Sketch

Q 3. Sketch the character of Mrs Ruffner.

श्रीमती रफनर का चरित्र चित्रण कीजिए।

कड़क मिजाज एवं अनुशासनप्रिय महिला – उन्हें संपूर्णता की आदत थी, जो व्यावहारिक रूप से संभव नहीं होता था – **उत्साहवर्द्धक व्यक्तित्व** – बुकर के काम से जब श्रीमती रफनर संतुष्ट रहने लगीं, वे उनकी शुभचिंतक हो गईं – उन्होंने बुकर को उनके लक्ष्य प्राप्ति हेतु प्रेरित करना शुरू कर दिया।

Ans. Mrs Ruffner was a very strict woman and she didn't get pleased easily.

We see the following traits in her character on the basis of this chapter

A Strict and Disciplined Woman Mrs Ruffner was a strict and disciplined woman that's why no one wanted to stay for long time as her servant. She did not get pleased easily so it was very tough to work for her. She wanted to see her house as a perfect place where everything remained in order.

A Motivator Mrs Ruffner was a perfect motivator also because when Booker joined her house and impressed her by his work, she became his well wisher and began to motivate him for achieving his goal which was to get admission in Virginia.

Thus, we see that Mrs Ruffner was a strict woman and a motivator also.

4

Helping Others

Booker Faced Scarcity of Money at the End of the First Year

After the first year ended, most of the students went home to spend their vacation, but Booker did not have enough money to go back home. He tried to sell his coat, but he was cheated by the man who bought it.

He then worked in a restaurant, but the owner cheated him. Finally, he landed at the house of the treasurer of the Hampton Institute, General JFB Marshall and explained his tough financial position to him. General Marshall put his faith in the young Washington and payed him the debt to re-enter the institute for the second year.

Booker Met with His Family Again

When the vacation period started once again at the end of the second year, Washington was able to go back home to Malden because of the money sent to him by his mother, his brother and also because of the generosity of his teachers.

Booker Joined School Before Reopening

Three weeks before the time of reopening of school, Booker received a letter from the head teacher Marry F Mackie, asking him to return as the building needed cleaning.

Booker jumped to the chance and reached Hampton. Booker worked very hard. When the Booker graduated from school, he was completely penniless.

4

Helping Others

प्रथम वर्ष की समाप्ति पर बुकर की दयनीय आर्थिक दशा

प्रथम वर्ष के अंत मे बहुत से विद्यार्थी छुट्टियाँ बिताने के लिए घर गए, परंतु पर्याप्त धन न होने के कारण Booker (बुकर) अपने घर नहीं गए। उन्होंने अपना कोट बेचने की कोशिश की, परंतु खरीदने वाले व्यक्ति द्वारा उन्हें धोखा मिला।

फिर उन्होंने एक Restaurant (भोजनालय) में काम किया, परंतु मालिक ने उन्हें धोखा दिया। अंततः वे Hampton Institute (हैम्पटन इंस्टीट्यूट) के Treasurer (कोषाध्यक्ष) General JFB Marshall (जनरल जे एफ बी मार्शल) के घर गए तथा उन्हें अपनी आर्थिक स्थिति के विषय में बताया। General Marshall (जनरल मार्शल) ने युवा वाशिंगटन पर विश्वास जताते हुए उन्हें पुनः द्वितीय वर्ष में प्रवेश हेतु debt (ऋण) दे दिया।

बुकर का अपने परिवार से दोबारा मुलाकात करना

द्वितीय वर्ष की समाप्ति के पश्चात् जब दोबारा छुट्टियाँ प्रारंभ हुई, तो अपनी माता तथा भाई के द्वारा भेजे गए धन की मदद से और अपने शिक्षकों की Generosity (दानशीलता) के कारण बुकर अपने घर वापस Malden (मालडेन) जाने में समर्थ हो गए।

बुकर विद्यालय खुलने से पूर्व विद्यालय में सम्मिलित हो गए

विद्यालय खुलने से तीन सप्ताह पूर्व ही बुकर को प्रधानाध्यापिका Marry F Mackie (मेरी एफ मैकी) का पत्र प्राप्त हुआ, जिसमें उन्होंने तत्काल विद्यालय भवन की सफाई की आवश्यकता का उल्लेख किया।

बुकर ने इस सुनहरे अवसर का लाभ उठाया तथा वे हैम्पटन पहुँच गए। बुकर ने कठिन परिश्रम किया। स्नातक हो जाने के बाद बुकर पूरी तरह से धनहीन थे।

Word Meaning

Confront	– सामना करना	Considerable	– उचित मात्रा में
Proprietor	– मालिक, स्वामी	Gratification	– कृतज्ञता
Content	– संतोष	Articulation	– सरल एवं सूक्ष्म वक्तव्य की कला
Pathetic	– दयनीय	Thrifty	– आर्थिक मामलों में सजग रहने वाला
Spur	– प्रेरणा, प्रोत्साहन	Dismal	– दु:खद, निराशाजनक
Elevation	– उत्थान	Disgrace	– लज्जा
Conduct	– आचरण, व्यवहार	Aspirations	– अभिलाषाएँ
Injured	– घायल	Race	– जाति
Elocution	– भाषण	Sermon	– नैतिक मुद्दा
Unpleasant	– निराशाजनक	Exist	– उपस्थित होना

Important Questions

Questions based on the Plot of the Chapter

Q 1. What were the financial constraints that stopped Booker from going back to his hometown at the end of the first year at Hampton?

किन आर्थिक मजबूरियों के कारण बुकर प्रथम वर्ष के समापन के पश्चात् हैम्पटन से घर वापस नहीं जा सके?

बुकर ने अपना अध्ययन प्रारंभ किया – प्रथम वर्ष समापन के पश्चात् गर्मी की छुट्टियाँ होना – धन के अभाव के कारण बुकर का अपने घर नहीं जाना – घर जाने हेतु धन के लिए बुकर ने अत्यधिक प्रयत्न किए, परंतु उनका असफल होना – बुकर ने गर्मी की छुट्टियों में अपने व्यक्तित्व सुधार का कार्य किया – आर्थिक स्थिति अच्छी न होना – बुकर का खुश न होना।

Ans. When Booker started his studies at Hampton University, his financial condition was already pitiable. After the completion of the first year, there was summer vacation in his school and every student went to enjoy holidays, but Booker could not go anywhere as he was totally out of money. In order to arrange money, he sold his coat and worked in a hotel, but this did not help him.

Finally, he gave up the idea of going home and utilised his summer vacations in self improvement. Booker was not financially strong so he had to manage with all his requirements himself.

He wanted to meet his family members, but his financial condition did not allow him to do so. The travelling cost was quite high and at the end of the first year in Hampton Institute, he was almost penniless. He tried his best in order to arrange enough amount for going home, but he could not succeed in his efforts.

Booker was not happy with his situation, but he accepted the reality and tried to console himself as he was a very optimistic person.

Q 2. Who were Ku Klux Klan?

कु क्लक्स क्लैन कौन थे?

बुकर के समय नीग्रो जाति के लोगों से अत्यंत पक्षपातपूर्ण व्यवहार करना – गोरे लोगों का नीग्रो लोगों से दोयम दर्जे का व्यवहार करना – 'कु क्लक्स क्लैन' भी इसी प्रकार की एक संस्था थी – नीग्रो जाति के लोगों को स्थानीय राजनीति में महत्त्वपूर्ण पदों पर आने से रोकना – इस संस्था के लोगों में नीग्रो जाति के लिए अत्यंत घृणा एवं नफरत की भावना थी – बुकर इन सब से परिचित थे – अतः उन्होंने नीग्रो जाति को शिक्षित करने का निर्णय लिया।

Ans. The Era of Booker was not good for coloured people as they were not treated fairly by young white men. The 'Ku Klux Klan' were bands of white men, who had joined themselves together for the purpose of regulating the conduct of the Negro people.

The objective of 'Ku Klux Klan' members was also to prevent Negro people from exercising any influence in politics. The members of this band were very agressive and they had a feeling of dislike towards Negro people.

Booker was born in such an Era in which the people belonging to his race were treated very badly. Booker was aware of it that's why he wanted to make people educated. According to him, education was the only weapon to deal with all these types of problems.

The group of white men named 'Ku Klux Klan' was also following the same pattern in which Negro people were known as a symbol of inferiority.

5

The Reconstruction Period

Scope of Education in Reconstruction Phase

The period from 1867 to 1878 was the period of reconstruction for the Negro men. There were two problems that were constantly worrying the Negro people – One was of learning Greek and Latin language and the second was holding office. The ambition to secure education was more encouraging as the idea was that as soon as one gets a education, he could live without manual labour.

Biased Treatment Policy by Federal Government

Booker also highlighted another problem that was widespread during the reconstruction years was the dependence of the common people on the Federal Government for everything. In many cases, the ignorance of the Negroes was used to favour the white.

Moreover, there was an element in the North, which wanted to punish the Southern white men by forcing the Negroes into positions as the heads of the Southern white. They wanted to create animosity and gap between the two and the Negro people would always be at the receiving end.

Word Meaning

Prevalent	– प्रचलित	Supernatural	– अलौकिक
Glance	– झलक देखना	Squarely	– न्यायपूर्ण तरीके से
Alluring	– आकर्षक	Substantial	– विचारणीय
Mandate	– आदेश	Neighbourhood	– नजदीक

5

The Reconstruction Period

पुनर्निर्माण अवधि में शिक्षा का महत्त्व एवं संभावनाएँ

1867 से 1878 तक की अवधि को Negro (नीग्रो) जाति के लोगों के लिए पुनर्निर्माण अवधि माना गया। नीग्रो जाति के लोगों के समक्ष दो मुख्य समस्याएँ थीं, जो उन्हें हमेशा परेशान करती थीं – प्रथम, Greek and Latin (ग्रीक एवं लैटिन) भाषाओं को सीखना तथा द्वितीय, एक बेहतर कार्यक्षेत्र को चुनना। शिक्षा-प्राप्ति उनका मुख्य उद्देश्य था, क्योंकि उनकी सोच थी कि जितनी जल्दी वे शिक्षित होंगे उतनी ही जल्दी उन्हें मजदूरी से छुटकारा मिलेगा।

संघीय सरकार का पक्षपातपूर्ण रवैया

बुकर ने अन्य समस्याओं का गहन विश्लेषण किया तथा यह अनुभव किया कि पुनर्निर्माण अवधि के दौरान आम आदमी की संघीय सरकार पर निर्भरता अत्यधिक थी। अधिकतर मामलों में गोरे लोगों का पक्ष लिया जाता था तथा नीग्रो जाति की पूर्णतया उपेक्षा की जाती थी।

इसके अतिरिक्त North (उत्तरी) भाग में कुछ ऐसे तत्त्व भी थे, जो दक्षिण के गोरे लोगों को दंड देना चाहते थे, जिसके लिए उन्होंने नीग्रो जाति को South (दक्षिण) के गोरों का प्रमुख बना दिया। वे इन दोनों जातियों में शत्रुता तथा दरार पैदा करना चाहते थे और नीग्रो व्यक्ति सदैव कुछ प्राप्त करने की स्थिति में होते थे।

Morals	– जीवन के नैतिक मूल्य	Tremendous	– अत्यंत विशाल
Evasion	– टालना	Pursued	– जारी रखा गया
Inclined	– प्रवृत्त	Complimentary	– प्रशंसात्मक
Conceivable	– कल्पनीय	Agitating	– परेशान करने वाला मुद्दा

Important Questions

Questions based on the Plot of the Chapter

Q 1. What were Booker's views on the Negroes taking up teaching as profession?

नीग्रो जाति के जो लोग अध्यापन को व्यवसाय के रूप में अपना रहे थे, उनके विषय में बुकर के क्या विचार थे?

पुनर्निर्माण अवधि के दौरान नीग्रो जाति के लोग शिक्षित हो रहे थे – शिक्षा के बढ़ते प्रचलन के कारण शिक्षक होना एक आकर्षण युक्त विकल्प होने लगा – बुकर ने नीग्रो जाति के लोगों द्वारा शिक्षक व्यवसाय चुनने के निर्णय को सही माना – शिक्षक अपने ओहदे की सुरक्षा हेतु अपने अनुयायियों के अनुसार पढ़ाया करते थे – बुकर का सुनिश्चित करना कि शिक्षक व्यवसाय में आने वाले लोग दूसरों को प्रशिक्षण देने योग्य हैं भी या नहीं।

Ans. During the time of reconstruction, Negro people were being educated and seeking for a suitable profession with respect also. Because of an increase in awareness towards education, teaching became a suitable and lucrative profession for Negro people at that time.

Booker appreciated Negro people for their taking up teaching as a profession, but there was a lack of quality of teaching as most of the teachers were a little educated only. In addition to this, they did not apply their own conception and continued teaching according to their supporters in order to protect their positions.

Booker was much aware of the importance of education. He wanted to make every student educated so that the society could become more developed.

Booker wanted to be sure that the persons, who got involved in profession of educating others must be wise and enough capable of training others. In the Era of Booker, people started to opt teaching as a profession in a large number because it was a respectful and safe profession.

Q 2. Did Booker disapprove of the way Negro people behaved towards the Central Government? What did he feel about functioning of the Central Government to uplift the Negro race?

क्या बुकर ने नीग्रो जाति के लोगों के संघीय सरकार के प्रति व्यवहार को अनुचित ठहराया? सरकार के नीग्रो जाति के सुधार के प्रयासों पर उनकी क्या प्रतिक्रिया थी?

बुकर ने अनुभव किया कि नीग्रो जाति के लोगों का संघीय सरकार में आने का प्रयत्न करना – बुकर का नीग्रो जाति के लोगों के संघीय सरकार के प्रति रवैये से आंशिक रूप से सहमत होना – संघीय सरकार का भी नीग्रो जाति के लोगों के उत्थान हेतु कार्य करना – नीग्रो लोगों की सुरक्षा तथा बेहतर विद्यालयों का प्रबंध भी करना – परंतु अभी बहुत कुछ किया जाना बचा था।

Ans. Booker felt that a large number of Negro people wanted to join parliamentary positions in order to make themselves more secure. All Negro people were not deserving candidates for membership of parliament, but there were various earnest and deserving Negro persons also.

Booker was partially agree with the behaviour of Negro people towards Federal Government. The Federal Government was taking steps to improve the life of Negro people, but efforts were not sufficient.

Federal Government provided Negro people protection and public schools were set-up for Negro people, but a lot of work was left to be done. Booker knew that securing a safe and powerful position in government was dream of everybody at that time. There were some restrictions also because of old traditions, but the Negro people were not deserving candidates because most of them were uneducated till that time.

On the other hand, Federal Government tried to make the position of Negro people much better by providing them better opportunities, but the progress was slow.

6

Black Race and Red Race

Booker's Entering Politics

Booker campaigned for the capital of West Virginia voting, which made him an effective speaker. Many friends and relatives insisted Booker to join politics. But he wanted to do something where he could help the Negro race to improve their poor condition.

Booker Became an Inspiring Educationist

Booker got surprised and happy to receive a letter from General Armstrong inviting him to Hampton to deliver the Post-Graduate speech during degree conferring ceremony. He accepted it and his speech entitled 'The Force that Wins' received a thunderous applause.

Booker Influenced Red Indians

For the first, General Armstrong decided to educate Red Indians at Hampton. He reserved one hundred seats for wild and ignorant Red Indians. Booker took the charges of seventy five Red Indians youth.

Booker Guided Students at Night-School

Booker T Washington was given another job at the end of his first year of working at Hampton. This was to teach children who had no means of paying for education and lodging. His job was to see that they worked for ten hours and attended the night-school for two hours. Men had to work in a saw mill and women in a laundry. He claimed that these poor students were so hard working and sincere to their studies that he called them 'The Plucky Class'. Later, 25 students from night-school went on to hold important positions all through the South America.

6

Black Race and Red Race

बुकर का राजनीति में प्रवेश

Booker (बुकर) ने West Virginia (पश्चिमी वर्जिनिया) की राजधानी के लिए होने वाले मतदान का प्रचार किया, जिससे वे एक कारगर वक्ता बन गए। बुकर के बहुत से मित्रों तथा संबंधियों ने उन्हें राजनीति में जाने की सलाह दी, परंतु बुकर कुछ ऐसा करना चाहते थे, जिससे वे Negro (नीग्रो) जाति के लोगों की दयनीय दशा को सुधार सकें।

बुकर एक प्रेरक शिक्षाविद् हो गए

बुकर बहुत खुश हुए जब उन्हें General Armstrong (जनरल आर्मस्ट्रांग) का पत्र प्राप्त हुआ, जिसमें Hampton (हैम्पटन) में उपाधि वितरण के दौरान उन्हें स्नातकोत्तर भाषण देने का निमंत्रण था। उन्होंने इस निमंत्रण को स्वीकार कर लिया और उनके The Force that Wins (द फोर्स डेट विंस) नामक शीर्षक युक्त प्रभावी भाषण को अत्यंत सराहा गया।

बुकर ने रेड इंडियंस को प्रभावित किया

जनरल आर्मस्ट्रांग ने पहली बार यह निर्णय लिया कि वे हैम्पटन में Red Indian (रेड इंडियन) को भी पढ़ाएँगे। उन्होंने जंगली और अज्ञानी रेड इंडियन के लिए एक सौ सीटें आरक्षित कर दीं। बुकर ने 75 जवान रेड इंडियन की जिम्मेदारी ले ली।

बुकर ने रात्रिकालीन विद्यालय में छात्रों का मार्गदर्शन किया

हैम्पटन में काम करते हुए प्रथम वर्ष के अंत में बुकर टी वाशिंगटन को एक और कार्य दिया गया। यह कार्य उन छात्रों को शिक्षित करना था, जो शिक्षा तथा रहने का खर्च व्यय नहीं कर पाते थे। उनका कार्य यह देखना था कि छात्र दस घंटे काम करके दो घंटे रात्रिकालीन विद्यालय में अध्ययन करें। आदमी को Saw Mill (आरा मिला) एवं महिलाओं को धोबीघाट पर काम करना पड़ता था। वे दृढ़तापूर्वक मानते थे कि वे गरीब बच्चे अत्यधिक परिश्रमी तथा ईमानदार थे और उन्होंने उन्हें The Plucky Class ('द प्लकी क्लास') नाम दिया। बाद में रात्रिकालीन विद्यालय के 25 छात्रों का South America (दक्षिणी अमेरिका) में विभिन्न महत्त्वपूर्ण पदों पर चयन हो गया।

Word Meaning

Invitation	– निमंत्रण	Permanent	– स्थायी
Preferment	– पदोन्नति	Determination	– दृढ़ निश्चय
Surprise	– आश्चर्य	Trasverse	– यात्रा करना
Solely	– अकेले	Mould	– परिवर्तन
Dreaded	– भयभीत	Cautiously	– सावधानीपूर्वक
Resent	– असहमत होना	Inflict	– प्रभावित करना
Amusing	– आनन्ददायक	Criticise	– आलोचना करना
Complexion	– त्वचा का रंग	Prudent	– बुद्धिमान
Position	– पद	Department	– विभाग

Important Questions

Questions based on the Plot of the Chapter

Q 1. What title did Booker give to his first speech at Hampton Institute? How was it received by his audiences?

बुकर ने किस शीर्षक से अपना प्रथम भाषण हैम्पटन इंस्टीट्यूट में दिया? उस पर लोगों की क्या प्रतिक्रियाएँ रहीं?

जनरल आर्मस्ट्रांग का बुकर को हैम्पटन इंस्टीट्यूट के छात्रों को संबोधित करने का निमंत्रण देना – बुकर का अत्यंत प्रसन्न होना – सावधानी के साथ अपने भाषण की रचना करना द फोर्स डेट विंस नामक शीर्षक पर भाषण देना – बुकर का हैम्पटन इंस्टीट्यूट वापस आना – उनकी पुरानी स्मृतियों का फिर से जी उठना – सभी छात्र-छात्राओं एवं अध्यापकों द्वारा उनका स्वागत करना – उनकी सराहना करना – भाषण का ओजपूर्ण एवं प्रेरक होना – बुकर का अनेक कठिनाइयों का सामना करना।

Ans. General Armstrong invited Booker to deliver a speech at Hampton Institute and Booker became very happy on his proposal. He prepared his speech with extreme care and he decided to give it the title The Force that Wins.

When he returned to Hampton Institute, his olden memories revived again. All students and teachers bacame very happy and surpriesd. Booker was warmly welcomed by everyone.

Finally, when he delivered his speech, everyone appreciated it as it was quite inspiring and energetic which was the requirement of students at that stage of their life.

In addition to this, Booker himself faced various challenges in his life, which also helped him in preparing an effective speech. When Booker delivered his carefully prepared content to the fresh graduates, they accepted it with a great enthusiasm.

Questions based on the Character-Sketch

Q 2. Draw the character-sketch of the poor students, at the night school, called as 'The Plucky Class'.

रात्रिकालीन विद्यालय के गरीब छात्र-छात्राओं, जिन्हें 'बहादुर समूह' का नाम दिया गया था, के चरित्र की क्या विशेषताएँ थीं?

आशावादी छात्र – छात्राओं की आर्थिक दशा अत्यंत खराब होना – समाज में अत्यंत निचले स्तर का होना – शिक्षित होने के लिए अत्यधिक जुनून का होना – अपने भविष्य के प्रति अत्यंत आशावित होना।

Ans. The Plucky Class was the group of poor coloured children, who wanted to become educated.

On the basis of this chapter, we see following traits in their characteristic

Optimistic The students of this group were not economically well. they, were ignorant of society, but they had a hope for better future that's why they wanted to become educated. This was a typical task, but they worked their best to accomplish this task successfully.

Bright and Assiduous Those students were very hard working and bright because they managed their schedule for ten hours working during day and then they attended two hours schooling during night. That's why they were termed as 'The Plucky Class' by Booker, who was the mentor of this group.

7

Early Days at Tuskegee

General Armstrong Suggested Booker's Name for Post of Teacher

During giving training to Red Indians in Hampton, Booker himself used to study. One day in assembly when the prayer was over, General Armstrong told Booker T Washington that a man in Albama wanted someone from white race to take charge of a normal school for Negro people at Tuskegee.

But General Armstrong told that man that a Negro man should be given the responsibility of the school. The General endorsed Booker and he was hired to look after Tuskegee school in June, 1881.

Government Released Fund for School

Booker was pleased to see the normal ease with which all races resided in the town. The legislature of Albama granted an annual fund of $ 2000, but this money could be used only to pay the salaries of the teachers. There was no provision for any land, building or apparatus.

Word Meaning

Secured	– प्राप्त किया	Inhabitant	– निवासी
country	– राज्य का छोटा-सा हिस्सा	Distinguish	– पहचानना
Expect	– उम्मीद करना	Costly	– महँगा
Supply	– आपूर्ति	Ideal	– आदर्श
Apparatus	– उपकरण	Secluded	– अकेला

7

Early Days at Tuskegee

जनरल आर्मस्ट्रांग ने अध्यापक पद हेतु बुकर का नाम सुझाया

हैम्पटन में Red Indians (रेड इंडियंस) को प्रशिक्षित करने के दौरान Booker (बुकर) स्वयं भी अध्ययन किया करते थे। एक दिन General Armstrong (जनरल आर्मस्ट्रांग) ने सभागार में प्रार्थना समाप्त होने के पश्चात् बुकर को बताया कि Albama (अलबामा) प्रांत के एक व्यक्ति ने उनसे Tuskegee (टस्कजी) प्रांत में Negro (नीग्रो) जाति के बच्चों के विद्यालय के लिए किसी गोरे अध्यापक की माँग की है।

परंतु जनरल आर्मस्ट्रांग ने उस व्यक्ति को बताया कि नीग्रो जाति के एक व्यक्ति को विद्यालय की जिम्मेदारी दे दी जाए। जनरल ने बुकर का नाम निश्चित कर दिया और जून, 1881 में उन्हें टस्कजी विद्यालय में संपूर्ण देख-रेख के लिए नियुक्त कर दिया गया।

सरकार ने विद्यालय के लिए धनराशि जारी कर दी

बुकर को अच्छी अनुभूति हुई, जब उन्होंने देखा कि कस्बे में सभी जाति के लोग परस्पर मिलकर रह रहे थे। अलबामा के प्रशासन ने विद्यालय के लिए $ 2000 की वार्षिक निधि जारी की, परंतु इतनी रकम में मात्र अध्यापकों का मासिक वेतन ही दिया जा सकता था। भूमि, भवनों अथवा उपकरणों हेतु किसी प्रकार की सहायता राशि नहीं थी।

Advantage	– लाभ	Prejudice	– भेदभाव
Regularly	– नियमित रूप से	Privilege	– सम्मान
Devotional	– आध्यात्मिक	Pleasure	– आनंद
Inspiring	– प्रेरणादायी	Inspiring	– प्रेरणादायी
Surprise	– आश्चर्य	Disappointment	– निराशा

Important Questions

Questions based on the Plot of the Chapter

Q 1. What was the new assignment given to Washington after completing one year at night-school? Why did he find this task as making bricks without straw?

रात्रिकालीन विद्यालय में एक वर्ष पूरा करने के पश्चात् बुकर को कौन-सा नया काम मिला? उन्हें यह काम मुश्किल क्यों प्रतीत हुआ?

बुकर को अलबामा में नीग्रो जाति के विद्यार्थियों के विद्यालय में पढ़ाने का कार्य देना – विद्यालय का अलबामा के निकट टस्कजी में होना – सरकार द्वारा विद्यालय को $ 2000 की सहायता राशि प्रदान करना – बुकर द्वारा कम धन को बराबर रूप से विभिन्न मदों में विभाजित करना असम्भव होना – बुकर द्वारा अनुभवी होना।

Ans. After completion of one year at night-school, Booker was assigned a new task of playing the role of a teacher at an institute for coloured people in Albama. The school was situated at Tuskegee near Albama.

But there was a various problems with the school like lack of apparatus, scarcity of proper infrastructure and so on. The government decided to release a fund of $ 2000 for the school which was not sufficient for school.

Booker had to manage everything as he was head of the school. Using such less amount effectively for equal allocation was next to impossible so Booker seemed this task like making bricks without straw.

Booker knew that without availability of sufficient infrastructure, it was impossible to provide better training to the students. The infrastructural strength of the institute at Albama was not satisfactory which was a point of disappointment for Booker, but Booker was an experienced person.

When he observed the overall situation of that institute, he began to frame plans for development of institute.

Questions based on the Character-Sketch

Q 2. Draw the character-sketch of Booker as an educational leader with courage to fight against adversities.

कई विषमताओं से सफलतापूर्वक निपटते हुए बुकर ने जो शिक्षा का प्रसार किया उस आधार पर उनकी चारित्रिक विशेषताओं का वर्णन कीजिए।

बुकर का सभी को शिक्षा एवं इसके महत्त्व से अवगत कराना – उनके समय में उनके लिए अपने उद्देश्य को पाना आसान कार्य न होना – लक्ष्य से अपना ध्यान न भटकाना – बुकर का प्रगतिवादी विचारधारा का होना – बुकर का शिक्षित होना – प्रसिद्ध शिक्षक का होना – बुकर में दृढ़निश्चयता का होना।

Ans. Booker always tried to make everyone aware of importance of education. His life was an example of struggle and bravery. In the Era of Booker, situation was quite difficult for fulfilment of his purposeE but he fought against all problems and did whatever he wanted.

On the basis of this chapter, we see following traits in his character

A Determined Person Booker had various problems including his familiar problems, problems in his society, racism etc but inspite of all these difficulties, he never missed his focus and kept trying to do whatever he wanted.

A Progressive Thinking Person Booker was educated so he understood the importance of being educated. That's why he always tried to make everyone aware of education and its importance.

A Popular Teacher He was a popular teacher also because whereever he went to teach, he got a warmly welcome by everybody because of his best characteristics.

Thus, it can be said that Booker was a determined person and popular teacher with a progressive thinking.

8

Teaching School in a Stable and a Hen-House

Booker Decided to Open a School

Booker travelled through Albama where he saw the miserable condition of people, which left him quite pitiful. He resolved to start a quality school for the Negro children and the school was finally opened on July 4, 1881. The white men questioned the wisdom of starting the school. They thought if Negroes are educated, there would be scarcity of domestic servants and workers on their farms. But Booker got help from a white man, Mr George W Campbell and a black ex-slave Mr Lewis Adams who helped him a lot in setting up the school.

Booker Arranged a Proper Building for the School

The need for a proper building for the school was growing day by day. That entire space cost them $500, which Booker did not have. He wrote to General Marshall, the treasurer of Hampton Institute, who readily agreed to give him a loan from his own funds.

Repayment of Loan was a Typical Task

Although, the school was making significant progress, the loan repayment was still a major problem. Miss Davidson organised festivals and suppers and quite a little sum of money was raised. People came forward as per their capacity. Since Booker started working at Tuskegee, he received many gifts for the school.

8

Teaching School in a Stable and a Hen-House

बुकर ने एक विद्यालय खोलने का निर्णय लिया

Booker (बुकर) ने Albama (अलबामा) का भ्रमण किया जहाँ उन्हें लोगों की दयनीय दशा का पता चला, जिससे उन्हें अत्यंत कष्ट हुआ। उन्होंने Negro (नीग्रो) जाति के छात्रों हेतु एक गुणवत्तायुक्त विद्यालय खोलने का निर्णय लिया और अंततः 4 जुलाई, 1881 को उन्होंने विद्यालय खोल दिया। गोरे लोगों ने विद्यालय खोलने की गंभीरता पर कई सवाल उठाए। उन्हें भय था कि यदि नीग्रो जाति के लोग शिक्षित होने लगेंगे तो घरेलू नौकरों की तथा उनके खेतों में काम करने वालों की कमी होने लगेगी, परंतु बुकर ने एक गोरे व्यक्ति Mr George W Campbell (श्रीमान जॉर्ज डब्ल्यू कैंपबेल) एवं एक भूतपूर्व गुलाम Mr Lewis Adams (श्रीमान लुईस एडम्स) से सहायता प्राप्त की, जिन्होंने विद्यालय स्थापना में उनकी अत्यधिक मदद की।

बुकर ने विद्यालय हेतु उचित भवन का प्रबंध किया

विद्यालय हेतु नए भवन परिसर की आवश्यकता दिन-प्रतिदिन बढ़ती जा रही थी। उस संपूर्ण जगह की कीमत $ 500 थी तथा इतनी रकम बुकर के पास नहीं थी। उन्होंने Hampton Institute (हैम्पटन इंस्टीट्यूट) के कोषाध्यक्ष General Marshall (जनरल मार्शल) को पत्र लिखा जो तुरंत स्वयं के कोष से ब्याज पर रकम देने हेतु तैयार हो गए।

ब्याज की रकम लौटाना एक मुश्किल कार्य था

यद्यपि विद्यालय भलीभाँति उन्नति के पथ पर अग्रसर था, परंतु ब्याज की रकम लौटाना अभी भी एक मुश्किल कार्य साबित हो रहा था। Miss Davidson (मिस डेविडसन) ने कार्यक्रमों का आयोजन कराया, जिससे अत्यंत कम धन का प्रबंध हुआ। लोगों ने अपनी-अपनी क्षमतानुसार आर्थिक मदद दी। जब से बुकर ने टस्कजी में कार्य करना प्रारंभ किया था, तब से उन्हें स्कूल के लिए कई उपहार मिले थे।

Word Meaning

Confess	– स्वीकार करना	Imitate	– नकल करना
Disfavour	– असहमति	Wits	– सामान्य बुद्धि
Undertaking	– कार्य	Vain	– व्यर्थ हो जाना
Derive	– व्युत्पन्न	Reliable	– विश्वसनीय
Registering	– पंजीकरण करना	Smattering	– अल्पज्ञान होना
Ignorant	– अल्पज्ञानी	Vice	– बुरी आदत
Normal	– सामान्य	Instructor	– निर्देश देने वाला
Epidemic	– बीमारी का तीव्र प्रसार	Generosity	– उदारता
Deceive	– धोखा देना	Apparent	– स्पष्ट रूप से दिखने वाला

Important Questions

Questions based on the Plot of the Chapter

Q 1. Why did some of the whites opposed the concept of a new school for the coloured race?

कुछ गोरे व्यक्तियों ने नीग्रो जाति के लिए विद्यालय की अवधारणा का विरोध क्यों किया?

बुकर का नीग्रो जाति के लोगों हेतु एक विद्यालय खोलने का निर्णय लेना – गोरे व्यक्तियों का विरोध करना – नीग्रो जाति के लोगों का सामूहिक रूप से शिक्षित होना – गोरे लोगों की आर्थिक स्थिति एवं आर्थिक महत्त्व में कमी आना – गोरे लोगों का यह सोचना कि शिक्षा प्राप्ति के बाद नीग्रो खेतों में काम करना छोड़ देंगे।

Ans. Booker decided to open a new school for Negro people at Tuskegee, but some white people opposed his concept because they were racists and they had a fear that it might result in bringing about trouble between races.

Besides, white people were also anxious about their economic degradation after mass education of Negro people. White people opposed the concept of school for Negro because they feared that the result of education would induce Negro people to leave farming works which would create difficulty for white people to find out domestic servants also. White people were very cruel and biased for Negro people. They did not want to let Negro people developed because they wanted to continue their use as slaves and domestic servants.

Questions based on the Character-Sketch

Q 2. Give a character-sketch of Miss Davidson with reference to her services to the school.

मिस डेविडसन की विद्यालय के प्रति दी गई सेवाओं के आधार पर उनका चरित्र चित्रण कीजिए।

मिस डेविडसन एक दयालु युवती – नीग्रो जाति का प्रयत्नशील होना – सहायक चिकित्सक की भूमिका निभाना – युवा पीढ़ी को अधिक-से-अधिक शिक्षित एवं जिम्मेदार बनाना – पूर्व में मिसिसिपी की अध्यापिका रहना।

Ans. Miss Davidson was a sincere lady who wanted to do something for upliftment of Negro race. She was a kind lady.

On the basis of this chapter, we see following traits in her character

A Benevolent Lady Miss Davidson was a benevolent lady because she wanted to do something for the upliftment of Negro race. She was previously employed as a nurse, then she became a teacher at Mississippi, but she was not satisfied. She wanted to contribute more for the progress of black race.

Careful and Responsible Lady Miss Davidson was a careful and responsible lady, because when she joined the school at Tuskegee, she fully devoted herself in teaching students. She did not opt the teaching profession for earning money, but she wanted to make younger generation more and more educated.

A Bold Lady Miss Davidson was a bold lady, because she decided to take various steps for arranging the money so that the debt could be repay.

Thus, we see that Miss Davidson was a benevolent, bold and careful lady with responsible attitude.

9

Anxious Days and Sleepless Nights

Strange Christmas Celebration

The people of Tuskegee wasted there Christmas week in drinking, partying and using guns and pistols indiscriminately. People never understood the true meaning of the festival. One Negro man told Booker that God cursed labour, hence they lived this holiday week happily because it was free from sin.

Students Celebrated Christmas Meaningfully

In the school, lessons were taught to the students to observe Christmas with dignity and they celebrated it in an unselfish way, doing service to the mankind. They interacted so well with the community and at the end of 3 months, they were able to pay the loan of $ 250 to General Marshall and within 2 months more had secured $ 500 and received a deed of the 100 acre land.

Booker Tried to Give His Best

The students were constantly growing in numbers. They needed a large solid building which would have cost about $ 6000. It was a huge sum. A Southern white man came forward and insisted on putting timber for the building and did not expect immediate cash. Miss Davidson arranged small contributions. People came forward and manually laboured. The first proper building came up and was named Porter Hall, after Mr A H Porter of Brooklyn, New York who gave a generous sum towards its errection. Two ladies from Boston offered $ 400 to the school.

9

Anxious Days and Sleepless Nights

क्रिसमस पर्व मनाने का विचित्र तरीका

Tuskegee (टस्कजी) के लोग Christmas (क्रिसमस) का पूरा सप्ताह मदिरापान, हथियारों एवं बंदूकों का प्रयोग करते हुए गँवा देते थे। वे लोग कभी भी इस त्यौहार का वास्तविक अर्थ नहीं समझ सके। बुकर को एक वृद्ध नीग्रो व्यक्ति ने बताया कि भगवान ने मजदूरी को अभिशाप घोषित किया, क्योंकि यह पापों से मुक्त थी। अत: वे लोग यह पूरा सप्ताह बिना मजदूरी किए प्रसन्नतापूर्वक बिताया करते थे।

विद्यार्थियों ने क्रिसमस पर्व अर्थपूर्ण विधि से मनाया

विद्यार्थियों ने क्रिसमस को स्वार्थहीन रूप से मानवता की सेवा करते हुए मनाने का निर्णय किया, क्योंकि उन्हें विद्यालय में इसका महत्त्व बताया गया था। वे सभी से प्रेमपूर्वक मिले और 3 महीनों के पश्चात् उनके पास Gneral Marshall (जनरल मार्शल) को लौटाने हेतु $ 250 की रकम हो गई थी तथा अगले 2 महीनों में उन्होंने $ 500 का इंतजाम करके 100 एकड़ भूमि ले ली।

बुकर ने अपना सर्वश्रेष्ठ देने का प्रयास किया

विद्यार्थियों की संख्या में लगातार वृद्धि हो रही थी। अब उन्हें एक बड़े मजबूत भवन की आवश्यकता हुई, जिसकी कीमत लगभग $ 6000 थी। यह बहुत बड़ी रकम थी। एक दक्षिण क्षेत्र का गोरा व्यक्ति आगे आया और उसने भवन के लिए लकड़ियाँ देने का प्रस्ताव रखा तथा उसने तत्काल लकड़ियों का दाम भी लेने से मना कर दिया। Miss Davidson (मिस डेविडसन) ने भी कुछ धन का प्रबंध किया। लोग आगे आए और शारीरिक रूप से श्रमदान किया। प्रथम इमारत बनकर तैयार हुई, जिसका नाम Porter Hall (पोर्टर हॉल) रखा गया, जोकि Brooklyn (ब्रुकलिन), New York (न्यूयॉर्क) के Mr A H Porter (श्रीमान ए एच पोर्टर) के नाम पर था, जिन्होंने भवन निर्माण में अपना बहुमूल्य योगदान दिया था। Boston (बोस्टन) से दो युवतियों ने भी विद्यालय को $ 400 की सहायता दी थी।

A Pathetic Chapter of Booker's Life

During the summer of 1882, Booker got married to Miss Fannie Smith. After earnest and constant work in the school, together with her house keeping duties, she passed away in May, 1884 leaving one daughter behind, Portia M Washington. Booker was completely shattered because of her wife's untimely death.

बुकर के जीवन का एक दु:खद अध्याय

1882 ई. की गर्मियों में बुकर का विवाह Miss Fannie Smith (मिस फैनी स्मिथ) से हुआ। विद्यालय में परिश्रमपूर्वक कार्य करते हुए और अपनी घरेलू जिम्मेदारियों को पूरा करते हुए उनका मई, 1884 में देहांत हो गया एवं वे अपने पीछे एक पुत्री Portia M Washington (पोर्शिया एम वाशिंगटन) को छोड़ गईं। अपनी पत्नी के असमय निधन से बुकर अत्यंत दु:खी हो गए।

Word Meaning

Difficult	– कठिन	Hilarity	– उल्लास की भावना
Sacredness	– पवित्रता	Preacher	– धर्मशिक्षक
Satisfactory	– संतोषजनक	Determined	– दृढ़प्रतिज्ञ
Stake	– जोखिम	Permanent	– स्थायी
Settlement	– सुलह, शांति	Lumber	– लकड़ी के हिस्से
Contribution	– योगदान	Conversation	– वार्तालाप
Strength	– ताकत	Acute	– अति आवश्यक
Gloomy	– उदासी भरा	Abolish	– हटा देना, समाप्त करना

Important Questions

Questions based on the Plot of the Chapter

Q 1. What did Booker observed in the Negro people celebrating Christmas holidays in a large plantation?

बुकर ने बड़े बगीचे में नीग्रो जाति के लोगों द्वारा क्रिसमस मनाने को लेकर क्या अनुभव किया?

↗ बुकर का क्रिसमस मनाते हुए लोगों को देखना – बडे बगीचे की तरफ जाना – बुकर द्वारा कई घरों में जाना – सीमित संसाधनों के बावजूद प्रसन्न रहना – पूरे परिवार के साथ त्यौहार मनाना।

Ans. Booker decided to visit the people celebrating Christmas, he went on a large plantation where he got various experiences. The people were very poor and in the situation of their poverty, they were trying to arrange some joy and happiness for themselves.

He visited various cabins where he saw different-different scenes, but one thing was common among those which was attempt of being happy inspite of scarcity of resources.

Moreover, Booker observed that people had ceased their work in the field and tried to lounge about their homes. Booker became very surprised because there were no prosperity in life of people at plantation, but they were trying to manage their happiness.

The optimistic approach of people impressed Booker very much and he became very happy after seeing this. People were enjoying and celebrating the festivities with full enthusiasm in presence of their family members. Thus, Booker observed the people and their Christmas celebration.

Q 2. How did the white community of Tuskegee react to Booker's decision to build a new building for the school?

विद्यालय के लिए नई इमारत बनाने को लेकर गोरे समुदाय के लोगों ने क्या प्रतिक्रिया दी?

बुकर का विद्यालय के लिए नया भवन बनाने का निर्णय लेना – गोरे संप्रदाय के लोगों से नकारात्मक प्रतिक्रिया मिलना – बुकर द्वारा अपने निर्णय पर अटल रहना – गोरे संप्रदाय के लोगों को समझाने का प्रयास करना।

Ans. When Booker decided to open a new building for the school he got negative responses from white community members. White, community treated Negro people in bad way, but Booker was determined so he decided to convince white community by making them aware of importance of equality.

He told them to co-operate in setting up of school and convinced them for understanding this as their own responsibility also. Booker believed in principle of equality and he tried to give his message to white community which worked successfully and finally they started favouring him.

Booker was against of any type of discrimination so he tried to convince white people regarding the necessity and importance of schools for Negro people.

10

Harder Task than Making Bricks without Straw

Booker Taught his Students the Lesson of Responsibility

Booker was striving to provide best possible education to his students, and under his able guidance, there was an-round development of students. Booker decided to teach his students to erect their own buildings, so that students had a feeling of pride and attachment. This way, the school would not only get the benefit of their efforts, but they themselves would be taught to see the utility in labour, beauty and dignity.

A Tough Assignment

During this time, Booker also decided to make bricks as there was no brickkilan nearby and there was a good demand of bricks in the market. Booker always sympathised with the children of Israel in their task of making bricks without straw, but the task of Booker and his student's was tougher.

Booker Got Credible Companions for School

Mr Bedford became the trustee of the school and worked for 18 years. Mr Logan looked after the school efficiently when Booker was away on tour to raise funds for the school. Whenever there was a need, students fulfill themselves on their own. Tuskegee now had a well cooked food served on tables with table clothes, meals on time.

10

Harder Task than Making Bricks without Straw

बुकर ने अपने विद्यार्थियों को जिम्मेदारी का पाठ पढ़ाया

Booker (बुकर) अपने छात्रों को यथासंभव उत्कृष्ट शिक्षा देने का प्रयास कर रहे थे, तथा उनके कुशल मार्गदर्शन में छात्रों का सर्वांगीण विकास हो रहा था। बुकर ने निर्णय लिया कि छात्रों को अपने लिए स्वयं भवन बनाने की शिक्षा दी जाए, जिससे छात्रों को गर्व व भावनात्मक संबंध महसूस होगा। इस प्रकार उनके परिश्रम से विद्यालय की उन्नति तो होगी ही साथ ही छात्रों में भी एकता की भावना तथा श्रम की महत्ता अनुभव करने की क्षमता का विकास होगा।

एक मुश्किल कार्य

बुकर ने इसी दौरान Bricks (ईंटें) बनाने का निर्णय लिया, क्योंकि उनके आस-पास के क्षेत्र में कोई ईंट बनाने का कारखाना नहीं था तथा बाजारों में ईंटों की अच्छी माँग थी। बुकर ने हमेशा Israel (इजरायल) के बच्चों की बिना तिनके से ईंटें बनाने की क्रिया से सहानुभूति रखी, परंतु बुकर तथा उनके छात्रों के लिए यह कार्य थोड़ा और मुश्किल था।

बुकर को विद्यालय हेतु विश्वसनीय साथी मिल गए

Mr Bedford (श्रीमान बेडफोर्ड) विद्यालय के समिति सलाहकार हो गए तथा लगभग 18 वर्षों तक उन्होंने विद्यालय के लिए कार्य किया। Mr Logan (श्रीमान लोगन) विद्यालय की जिम्मेदारी तब संभालते थे, जब बुकर विद्यालय हेतु धन जुटाने के लिए बाहर गए होते थे। जब भी कोई आवश्यकता होती थी, छात्र स्वयं उस आवश्यकता को पूरा करते थे। अब Tuskegee (टस्कजी) में भी भली-भाँति पकाया हुआ भोजन उपलब्ध होने लगा था, जिसे समय पर मेजपोश के साथ मेज पर पेश किया जाता था।

Word Meaning

Determined	– दृढ़निश्चयी	Nature	– व्यवहार
Assist	– सहायता करना	Civilisation	– सभ्यता
Erection	– उत्थान	Construct	– निर्माण करना
Valuable	– मूल्यवान	Temptation	– लालच
Connection	– जुड़ाव	Sympathised	– सहानुभूति व्यक्त की
Distate	– नफरत	Disgusted	– घृणित
Pleasant	– आनंददायक	Mould	– आकार देना
Difficult	– मुश्किल	Experiment	– प्रयोग
Troubles	– परेशानियाँ	Demoralised	– हतोत्साहित
Suitable	– उपयुक्त	Perhaps	– शायद, संभवत:
Benefactor	– मददगार	Eventually	– अंतत:
Objection	– विरोध	Obliterate	– नष्ट कर देना

Important Questions

Questions based on the Plot of the Chapter

Q 1. Why did Booker want students to errect the school building by their manual labour? How did this experience helped them in later stage of their career?

बुकर क्यों चाहते थे कि छात्र अपने लिए विद्यालय भवन का निर्माण स्वयं करें? बाद में छात्रों के जीवन में यह अनुभव किस काम आया?

छात्रों द्वारा भवन का निर्माण कराना – छात्रों को श्रम का महत्त्व बताना – विद्यालय को लाभ होना – छात्रों को सुंदरता का अनुभव कराना।

Ans. Booker wanted students to erect the school building by their manual labour because this would teach them the latest and best methods of labour. In addition to this, this would also be beneficial for the school and students would learn to see utility in labour with its beauty and dignity. He wanted to make them learn how labour could be lifted from drudgery and monotony. The experience of this work helped students in later stage of their life because they observed civilisation, self-help and self-reliance as an important part of life while doing this project.

Booker knew the importance of some qualities like-self-believe, self reliance etc. In life of everyone so he tried to make students work for their future prospects.

Students could not understand Booker's objective that's why they depicted repulsion but when Booker told them his objective in more clear way, they became very impressed by Booker's idea and worked according to his idea.

Q 2. What difficulties did Booker face while implementing the idea of brick-making at the school? How did this idea help the school financially?

ईंटें बनाने की योजना के क्रियान्वयन के दौरान बुकर को किन परेशानियों का सामना करना पड़ा? उनकी इस योजना ने विद्यालय की आर्थिक मदद कैसे की?

बुकर द्वारा टस्कजी में ईंटें बनाने का कारखाना खोलना – उद्देश्य पूरा करना – बुकर का लक्ष्य में सफल होना – छात्रों को ईंट बनाने के लिए प्रेरित करना – बाजार में ईंटों की माँग का होना।

Ans. Booker wanted to establish a brick making industry in tuskegee, but he had to face various challenges for his project like absence of required amount, lack of experienced, labourers etc.

Booker established a set-up for brick making, but the procedure of brick making was hard and dirty which forced many of the workers to leave the place and after it.

The kiln failed to work for 3 times. Inspite of such difficulties, Booker became successful in his project. Brick making helped the school very much because there was a good demand of bricks in the market and students sold their perfectly built bricks to arrange a good revenue for the school.

Booker executed the task of brick making with the help of his students. The prefect proved a tough task initially because of succeeded in his efforts.

In that area, there was a huge demand of bricks so by selling bricks, Booker became successful in collecting fund for the routine requirements of the school. Booker always tried to do best for his school.

11

Making their Beds before they could Lie on them

Booker's School Became Extremely Popular

Tuskegee Institute became so reputed that it started receiving famous people from Hampton. General Marshall, Mackie and General Armstrong of Hampton visited it. A number of teachers who had graduated from Hamptom Institute joined Booker's school. General Armstrong was welcomed by both the races.

Booker Taught the Lesson of Self Dependency

With the increase in the number of students, there was a pressing need for the institute to start their own boarding facility for the students. Booker told the students that the institute was not his, but it belonged to each and every student who studied there. This made quite an impact on the students and they at once got busy in making their own furniture.

Booker was Welcomed by the Whites

Industrial education became popular even among the whites. The understanding between the two races got cemented. The white people in and near Tuskegee seem to count it as a privilege to show all the respect within their power and often go out of their way to do this. On one occassion white ladies had requested Booker to have supper with him.

11

Making their Beds before they could Lie on them

बुकर का विद्यालय अत्यधिक प्रसिद्ध हो गया

Tuskegee (टस्कजी) के विद्यालय की प्रतिष्ठा इतनी बढ़ गई कि Hampton (हैम्पटन) से विख्यात लोग यहाँ आने लगे। हैम्पटन के General Marshall, Mackie and General Armstrong (जनरल मार्शल, मिस मैकी एवं जनरल आर्मस्ट्रांग) यहाँ आए। कई शिक्षकों ने, जो हैम्पटन इंस्टीट्यूट से स्नातक थे, बुकर के विद्यालय में प्रवेश लिया। जनरल आर्मस्ट्रांग का स्वागत दोनों जातियों ने किया।

बुकर ने आत्मनिर्भरता का सबक दिया

छात्रों की संख्या में लगातार वृद्धि होने के साथ विद्यालय में छात्रों के लिए Boarding Facility (छात्रावास सुविधा) की आवश्यकता और बढ़ रही थी। बुकर ने छात्रों से कहा कि विद्यालय केवल उनका ही नहीं, अपितु वहाँ के प्रत्येक छात्र का है, जो भी वहाँ अध्ययनरत है। इस बात का छात्रों पर गहरा प्रभाव पड़ा और वे अपने लिए फर्नीचर बनाने में लग गए।

गोरे व्यक्तियों ने भी बुकर का स्वागत किया

गोरे व्यक्तियों में भी औद्योगिक प्रशिक्षण की अवधारणा प्रसिद्ध हो गई। दोनों जातियों के मध्य मध्यस्थता गहरी होने लगी। गोरे व्यक्तियों ने नीग्रो जाति को सम्मान एवं विशेषाधिकार देने प्रारंभ कर दिए। एक अवसर पर गोरी महिलाओं ने बुकर से उनके साथ रात्रिभोज करने की प्रार्थना की।

Word Meaning

Encouraging	– उत्साहवर्द्धक	Rapid	– तीव्र
Welcome	– स्वागत	Generosity	– उदारता
Acquaintance	– मुलाकात	Prejudice	– भेदभाव
Contend	– संघर्ष	Provide	– उपलब्ध कराना
Confronting	– मुकाबला करना	Improve	– सुधार
Authority	– अधिकार	Contrive	– बनाना, उपाय निकालना
Flattery	– चापलूसी	Overseen	– देखभाल करने वाला
Marvel	– उत्कृष्ट	Absolute	– पूर्ण

Important Questions

Questions based on the Plot of the Chapter

Q 1. What lesson did Booker learnt from General Armstrong's behaviour towards both the races?

जनरल आर्मस्ट्रांग के दोनों जातियों के प्रति व्यवहार से बुकर को क्या सबक मिला?

जनरल आर्मस्ट्रांग का समानता का समर्थक होना – उनका व्यवहार प्रेरणादायक होना – बुकर द्वारा विद्यालय का भ्रमण करना – दोनों जातियों के लोगों द्वारा उनका गर्मजोशी से स्वागत करना – बुकर की पूर्व में ये धारणा कि जनरल आर्मस्ट्रांग का गोरे व्यक्तियों के प्रति कड़वे विचार रखना – व्यवहार को देखकर बुकर को अपनी भूल का अहसास होना – बुकर के लिए एक मूल्यवान सबक होना – बुकर ने आर्मस्ट्रांग की ये सीख हमेशा याद रखी कि अच्छे लोग सदा प्रेम भावना का प्रसार करते हैं, जबकि छोटी सोच वाले सदा नफरत का।

Ans. General Armstrong was a supporter of equality and his nature was very much inspiring. When he came to visit Booker's school, he received a warm welcome by both races which impressed Booker very much. Booker previously thought that General Armstrong had bitter thoughts for white race people, but he proved wrong when he saw the behaviour of him towards both races.

This was a precious lesson for Booker and he learned a lesson from General Armstrong that great men cultivate love and only little men cherish of hatred. Booker was also a supporter of equality and he did not believe in any kind of discrimination.

When Booker met with General Armstrong, he observed his behaviour and became inspired very much. General Armstrong himself was a great person and he had a better thought for everyone.

He received a warm welcome from both races and this impressed Booker very much. Thus, Booker also decided to gain same respect by harmonious views.

Questions based on the Character-Sketch

Q 4. Give a pen-portrait of the characteristic features of the students of Tuskegee school.

टस्कजी के विद्यालय के छात्रों की चारित्रिक विशेषताओं का वर्णन कीजिए।

छात्रों का उज्ज्वल एवं परिश्रमी होना उनका अपना ध्यान अपनी पढ़ाई पर लगाए रखना – अपने सुधार हेतु प्रयासरत रहना – केंद्रित एवं एकाग्रचित्त होना – संसाधनों की अनुपलब्धता के बावजूद बिना विरोध किए उनका अपने लक्ष्य में जुटे रहना – अपने अध्यापकों एवं बुकर की सीख का अनुसरण करना – अपने उज्ज्वल भविष्य की तरफ बढ़ना।

Ans. Students at Tuskegee school were very optimistic and hard working. They learned to adjust in every situation.

On the basis of this chapter, we see following traits in their character

Bright and Assiduous The students were bright and assiduous because they were paying their attention towards study and continuously trying to improve themselves.

Focused and Concentrated Those students were focused and concentrated because inspite of scarcity of enough resources, they continued their study without any complain or protest. They were planing and working hard for their better future by following their teacher and Mr Booker.

Thus, we can say that students at Tuskegee school were quite bright, assiduous, focused and concentrated.

12

Raising Money

Requirement of Accommodation for Girls

There arose the need to construct a larger building with another dormitory. Miss Davidson began a fund raising campaign and students began digging the foundation of another building. Miss Davidson appealed to both the races and they responded willingly in proportion to their means. But more was required.

General Armstrong Again Helped Booker

General Armstrong took Booker and a band of four singers to tour the North. Booker realised that this was his method of introducing him to the people of the North as well as raising funds for new school building.

Two years later, he received a contribution of $ 10000 from a man and $ 50000 from a couple. This was the great period in Booker's life, but he was under tremendous pressure to prove the efforts of Negro community.

Word Meaning

Preliminary	– प्रारंभिक	Ordinary	– सामान्य
Anxiety	– चिंता	Imagine	– कल्पना करना
Advancement	– वृद्धि	Proportion	– अनुपात
Cripple	– कमजोर करना	Condemned	– दोषी ठहराया हुआ
Persistent	– लगातार	Dignified	– सम्माननीय
Cordial	– मैत्रीपूर्ण	Conferred	– प्रदत्त
Impress	– प्रभावित करना	Arbour	– वृक्ष की लताएँ
Dawned	– दिमाग में बैठ जाना	Elevation	– उत्थान

12

Raising Money

छात्राओं हेतु निवास स्थान की आवश्यकता

वहाँ एक और विशाल शयनगार वाले भवन के निर्माण की आवश्यकता हुई। Miss Davidson (मिस डेविडसन) ने धन एकत्र करने हेतु अभियान आरंभ कर दिया तथा छात्रों ने दूसरी इमारत के लिए नींव की Digging (खुदाई) आरंभ कर दी। मिस डेविडसन ने दोनों जातियों से सहयोग की माँग की तथा उन्होंने स्वतंत्रतापूर्वक अपनी इच्छाओं के अनुरूप योगदान दिया। परंतु ज्यादा प्रयासों की आवश्यकता थी।

जनरल आर्मस्ट्रांग ने पुन: बुकर की मदद की

General Armstrong (जनरल आर्मस्ट्रांग) ने उत्तरी भाग की यात्रा के लिए Booker (बुकर) व चार गायकों के दल को अपने साथ ले लिया। बुकर ने उनके लिए अनुभव किया कि यह उत्तरी भाग में लोगों से संपर्क करने तथा अपने नए विद्यालय हेतु धन जुटाने का अच्छा तरीका था।

दो साल बाद उन्हें एक व्यक्ति द्वारा $ 10000 एवं एक दंपति द्वारा $ 50000 की सहायता राशि मिली। बुकर के जीवन का यह अत्यधिक सुखद अनुभव था, परंतु उन पर Negro (नीग्रो) जाति के प्रयत्नों को सिद्ध करने का दबाव भी था।

Dilapidated	– बुरी दशा में	Earnestness	– गंभीरता एवं सच्चाई
Provision	– प्रबन्ध	Luxury	– विलासिता की वस्तुएँ
Debt	– ऋण	Illustrating	– उदाहरण देना
Produce	– उत्पन्न करना	Community	– समुदाय, समूह विशेष
Worthless	– व्यर्थ, मूल्यहीन	Foundation	– आधारशिला
Simulated	– नकल किया हुआ	Philanthropic	– जिसमें लोकहित की भावना हो

Important Questions

Questions based on the Plot of the Chapter

Q 1. What was the plan of General Armstrong for raising funds for building Albama Hall at Tuskegee School?

टस्कजी विद्यालय में अलबामा हॉल की इमारत हेतु धन जुटाने के लिए जनरल आर्मस्ट्रांग की क्या योजना थी?

बुकर द्वारा विद्यालय में लड़कियों की बढ़ती संख्या को देखते हुए एक नई इमारत बनाने का निर्णय लेना – उनके द्वारा कार्य हेतु अभियान चलाकर धन एकत्रित करना – जनरल आर्मस्ट्रांग का एक संदेश भेजना – उत्तरी भाग में जाकर लोगों से धन एकत्र करने का प्रयास करने की योजना का उल्लेख होना – आर्मस्ट्रांग का बुकर एवं चार गायकों के समूह के साथ उत्तरी भाग में जाकर लोगों को समझाकर उनसे मदद लेने की योजना बनाना – बुकर के नए कार्य, 'अलबामा हॉल' हेतु अनुभवी आर्मस्ट्रांग की ये योजना लाभप्रद साबित हुई।

Ans. Booker felt the need of a new building as the number of girls was increasing in school. He decided to arrange money for this purpose by campaigning. Then, he received a telegram from General Armstrong in which he mentioned a scheme for collection of fund.

General Armstrong drafted a plan of going to the North part with Booker and a band of four singers in order to meet various people for fund collection purpose by convincing them.

General Armstrong was an experienced person and his plan was quite suitable for the accomplishment of the Booker's project named 'Albama Hall'.

General Armstrong was a perfect planner and he decided to help Booker in his goal achievement. General was ready to go with Booker because he was a generous and benevolent person and he also wanted to contribute in the holy mission of Booker. Booker became very happy and he became a little bit relaxed also because he was sure about the success of fund raising plan of General Armstrong.

Q 2. What principle did Booker followed in getting donations from the rich class?

धनी व्यक्तियों से दान लेने हेतु बुकर ने क्या सिद्धांत अपनाए?

बुकर द्वारा नई इमारत हेतु धन एकत्र करना – अतः उनके द्वारा उत्तर की यात्रा करना – वहाँ उनका सभी से मिलना तथा मदद का आह्वान करना – बुकर का स्वयं के लिए धन इकट्ठा नहीं करना – बुकर द्वारा एक सुरक्षित मार्ग स्वयं चुनना – लोगों से धन की याचना न करना – टस्कजी विद्यालय से जुड़े तथ्यों को प्रस्तुत करना – जिनके आधार पर उन्होंने धनी व्यक्तियों का विश्वास जीतने की कोशिश की – बुकर का सिद्धांतवादी व्यक्ति होना – अतः उन्होंने सदैव अपनी गरिमा के अनुरूप ही अपने कार्य किए।

Ans. Booker wanted to collect required amount for new building for which he travelled the North part. There, he met with everyone and tried to convince everyone for offering some help. Booker was not collecting money for own, so he was very confident. Booker followed a secure way of doing his work in which he never begged for money, but he presented facts related with Tuskegee School and tried to win support of rich persons on the basis of these facts. Booker was a man of principles that's why, he always tried to do his work with a dignity. Booker believed in charity work and he tried to do better for his school.

He was not economically enough strong so he decided to collect fund by campaigns and efforts for convincing others. He asked rich people also for money but he never requested them to do so, but he explained his vision in front of them in order to win their favour. He became successful in his mission and rich people also helped him a lot.

13

Two Thousand Miles for a Five-Minute Speech

More Students Got their Admission

There was a tremendous increase in the number of students who were worthy and intelligent, but who did not have money to pay even the small charges.

A night-school was started where students would attend 2 hours study at night, while working for 10 hours in day time. No student was allowed to take admission without physical labour.

Booker Selected his Life Partner

In 1885, Booker married Miss Olivia Davidson. Miss Olivia Davidson was largely responsible for the success of the school during its early history. She secured funds for school in various ways. She died in 1889, leaving two sons–Booker Taliaferro and Ernest Davidson.

Booker Got a Chance to Address People at National Level

It was the first time that Booker was called on to speak at the National Education Association in Boston and also invited to speak in the South. He travelled 2000 miles, made a five minutes speech to some influential people.

13

Two Thousand Miles for a Five-Minute Speech

अधिक छात्रों का प्रवेश

ऐसे विद्यार्थियों की संख्या तीव्रता से बढ़ रही थी जो योग्य एवं Intelligent (बुद्धिमान) तो थे, परंतु जिनके पास बहुत छोटे अभियोगों के लिए भी धन नहीं था।

Night School (रात्रिकालीन विद्यालय) का आरंभ किया गया। जहाँ छात्र 2 घंटे रात्रि में पढ़ाई करते थे तथा दिन में 10 घंटे काम किया करते थे। विद्यालय में ऐसे किसी भी छात्र को प्रवेश नहीं दिया जाता था, जो शारीरिक श्रम नहीं करते थे।

बुकर ने अपने लिए जीवन संगिनी चुन ली

1885 में बुकर ने Miss Olivia Davidson (मिस ओलिविया डेविडसन) से विवाह कर लिया। प्रारंभिक दिनों में स्कूल की सफलता के लिए मिस ओलिविया डेविडसन जिम्मेदार थीं। विद्यालय के लिए उन्होंने कई प्रकार से सहायता राशि एकत्रित की। 1889 में अपने दो बेटों Booker Taliaferro and Ernest Davidson (बुकर टेलियाफेरो एवं अर्नेस्ट डेविडसन) को छोड़कर वे मृत्यु को प्राप्त हो गईं।

बुकर को राष्ट्रीय स्तर पर लोगों को संबोधित करने का मौका मिला

यह पहला मौका था जब Boston (बोस्टन) प्रांत में आयोजित National Education Association (राष्ट्रीय शिक्षा समिति सम्मेलन) में लोगों को संबोधित करने हेतु तथा South (दक्षिण) भाग में भी भाषण हेतु बुकर को आमंत्रित किया गया। उन्होंने 2000 मील की यात्रा करके, कुछ प्रभावशाली लोगों के समक्ष पाँच मिनट का भाषण दिया।

Booker's Assignment was Tough and a Bit Complex

As Booker's engagements increased, he was aware that many whites were waiting for him to speak ill. That was true when he was called upon to deliver a speech at the opening of the Atlanta Cotton States and International Exposition on 18th September, 1895.

He spent a lot of time working on his speech, knowing that there were the Northern and the Southern whites and also Negroes among the audience, so the ennisons would be extremely sensitive.

बुकर के लिए मुश्किल कार्य

बुकर का व्यवसाय बढ़ता जा रहा था, उन्हें यह भी ज्ञात था कि बहुत से गोरे लोग उनके गलत भाषण की प्रतीक्षा कर रहे होंगे। यह सच भी हुआ, उन्हें Atlanta Catton States (अटलांटा कॉटन स्टेट्स) के अनावरण समारोह तथा International Exposition (अंतर्राष्ट्रीय प्रदर्शनी) में भाषण देने हेतु 18 सितंबर, 1895 को बुलाया गया।

उन्होंने बहुत-सा समय अपने भाषण की तैयारी करने में बिताया, क्योंकि उन्हें पता था कि वहाँ श्रोताओं में उत्तरी एवं दक्षिणी गोरे व्यक्तियों के साथ नीग्रो जाति के व्यक्ति भी रहेंगे तथा स्थान अत्यंत संवेदनशील रहेगा।

Word Meaning

Manual	– शारीरिक	Overlook	– देखने में अक्षम होना
Testify	– प्रमाण देना	Gratified	– संतुष्ट
Embitter	– असहनीय बना देना	Contend	– तथ्य देना
Confine	– सीमित कर देना	Ceaseless	– असीमित
Dominant	– महत्त्वपूर्ण	Influential	– प्रभावशाली
Misgiving	– शंका	Unanimous	– पूर्ण समर्थन
Creditable	– प्रशंसनीय	Prevailing	– सर्वव्याप्त
Intimation	– सूचना	Utterances	– भाषण
Flaring	– प्रभावी एवं बड़ा	Collapse	– थकान के कारण परस्त होना

Important Questions

Questions based on the Plot of the Chapter

Q 1. How did the audience react to Booker's first formal speech at the National Education Association?

राष्ट्रीय शिक्षा समिति में अपने पहले औपचारिक भाषण में बुकर को श्रोताओं ने क्या प्रतिक्रिया दी?

राष्ट्रीय शिक्षा समिति के सम्मेलन के दौरान बुकर का लोगों को संबोधित करना – बुकर का प्रथम औपचारिक भाषण देना – बुकर का श्रोताओं के समक्ष प्रभावी ढंग से अपनी बात को रखना – श्रोताओं में दोनों जातियों के व्यक्तियों का होना – भाषण की समाप्ति के पश्चात् लोगों द्वारा बुकर को प्रशंसात्मक प्रतिक्रियाएँ देना – लोगों का बुकर को धन्यवाद देना – बुकर का अपने भाषण में दक्षिणी गोरे व्यक्तियों द्वारा किए गए प्रशंसनीय कार्यों हेतु उन्हें श्रेय देना – बुकर ने अपने भाषण में कोई आपत्तिजनक अंश शामिल नहीं किया, जिससे श्रोता प्रभावित हुए।

Ans. Booker was invited to address the audience at the National Education Association where he delivered his first formal public speech. There were a number of audiences of mixed races and Booker delivered his speech without knowning this fact. After his speech, he received various positive remarks from audiences. Many audiences thanked him for giving credit to Southern white people for all praiseworthy things, they had done. Booker did not include any objectionable content in his speech which influenced his audiences too much.

Booker got a chance to address public of various races and he did not pass any negative remark during his addressing. The public accepted Booker's views and praised him very much. In addition to this, Booker was a person, who believed in promotion of goodness and truth.

He never underestimated the efforts of persons of any race which made him a real hero in public. Every person appreciated the speech delivered by Booker because everyone found his speech very much fair.

Q 2. What thing did Booker consider while preparing for his speech at various occasions?

बुकर विभिन्न अवसरों हेतु अपने भाषणों को तैयार करने में किन बातों का ध्यान रखते थे?

प्रथम औपचारिक भाषण के पश्चात् बुकर का एक कुशल वक्ता होना – सभी जातियों को संबोधित करना – कभी किसी जाति पर व्यंग्यात्मक टिप्पणी न करना – बुकर का सभी जातियों को समान मानना – उनका मानना था कि निंदा करके किसी में बदलाव नहीं लाया जा सकता – उसकी प्रशंसा अवश्य करना – बुकर का सभी उपायों द्वारा जातियों को परस्पर नजदीक लाने के प्रयत्न करना तथा उनमें मैत्रीपूर्ण संबंध स्थापित करने के प्रयास करना।

Ans. Booker became a public speaker after his first formal public speech. He oftenly addressed the audiences of various races, but he never became sarcastic towards any race.

He always equally treated every race and same was depicted in his public addressings. He believed that no one can be changed by abusing and if someone does some praiseworthy then one must be appreciated.

Booker always focused on bringing all races together and on cultivation of friendly relations by applying every honourable mean. Booker was a person, who remained diplomatic in his approach towards every race. He got various chances of addressing public which made him a skilful orator.

Booker always tried to connect with the heart of audiences so he became very successful in his public speaking art. Booker never tried to include any such part in his speeches which could harm sentiments of any race. This property of Booker helped him a lot in making him a lovable and effective speaker.

Q 3. What was the difference in speeches made by Booker to the Northern and the Southern states?

दक्षिणी भाग एवं उत्तरी भाग में बुकर व्दारा दिए गए भाषणों में क्या अंतर होता था?

बुकर का अत्यंत प्रसिद्ध होना – बुकर को लगभग सभी जातियों एवं प्रांतों के निवासियों को संबोधित करने का अवसर प्राप्त होना – बुकर को उत्तर एवं दक्षिण क्षेत्रों में भी भाषण देने का अवसर प्राप्त होना – दोनों स्थानों के लिए भिन्न-भिन्न नीतियाँ अपनाना – जब वे उत्तर क्षेत्र में गए तो उनका लोगों से विद्यालय हेतु और आर्थिक सहायता का आह्वान करना – विद्यालय की उन्नति हेतु उनके पूर्व प्रयासों को सराहा परंतु जब वे दक्षिण दिशा में गए तो उन्होंने अपने भाषण में लोगों से जातिवाद को जड़ से नाश करने का आह्वान किया तथा सभी के विकास हेतु सम्मिलित प्रयत्नों की आवश्यकता पर जोर दिया।

Ans. Booker was very famous and people wanted to hear him. Booker got chance to address almost every people irrespective of race, dwelling place, etc. Booker delivered his speeches in the North and the South both, but he followed different strategy during his addressings at both places.

When Booker addressed the Northern people, he tried to convince them for donating more for school by appreciation their previous efforts for betterment of school.

On the other hand, when Booker addressed the people of the South, he urged them to obliterate the evil practice of racism and to work together for the development and growth of everyone. Booker was a perfect judge also, who was very skilful in judging the mentality of his audiences.

He knew that during his campaign for school, he received help from every part of his state, so he decided to appreciate all of them. He did this in his speeches which became fruitful for him. He faced the audiences of different territories with different relevant issues and thus, his campaign became beneficial for the society.

14

The Atlanta Exposition Address

Booker Tried to Give a Harmonious Message

The Atlanta Expositions began with a short speech from Governor Bullock who introduced Booker as a representative of Negro enterprise and Negro civilization.

Booker Gave Same Message to Whites Also

Booker gave the same message to the whites. He asked them to cast down their buckets among those people who have, without strikes, cleared their forests, tilled their fields, build railroads and did numerous other things for the progress of the South.

Booker's Speech Created History

People were deeply influenced by Booker's speech. He got offers from publishers and speech circuits but he turned them down in favour of his work at Tuskegee. Some days later, Booker sent a copy of his speech to the President of the United States, the Hon. Grover Cleveland to which he also received an autographed reply.

14

The Atlanta Exposition Address

बुकर ने एक समतापूर्ण संदेश देने का प्रयास किया

Atlanta (अटलांटा) प्रदर्शनी की शुरूआत Governor Bullock (गवर्नर बुलक) के एक छोटे से भाषण से हुई, जिन्होंने Booker (बुकर) का परिचय Negro (नीग्रो) उद्योग तथा नीग्रो सभ्यता के प्रतिनिधि के रूप में कराया।

बुकर ने ऐसा ही संदेश गोरे व्यक्तियों को भी दिया

गोरे व्यक्तियों को भी बुकर ने यही संदेश दिया। बुकर ने उनसे कहा कि उन्हें नीग्रो जाति से भेदभाव नहीं करना चाहिए, जिन्होंने South (दक्षिण) के विकास के लिए जंगलों को काटा, खेतों को जोता, रेलवे के लिए पटरियाँ बिछाई एवं ऐसे ही अन्य बहुत से कार्य किए।

बुकर के भाषण ने इतिहास रच दिया

बुकर के भाषण ने जनमानस पर अत्यधिक प्रभाव डाला। उन्हें प्रकाशकों तथा अन्य संस्थाओं से अपने साथ जुड़ने का प्रस्ताव भी रखा, परंतु उन्होंने सारे प्रस्ताव ठुकराते हुए टस्कजी विद्यालय के लिए कार्य करते रहना जारी रखा। President of the United States, the Hon. Grover Cleveland (संयुक्त राष्ट्र के राष्ट्रपति मिस्टर ग्रोवर क्लीवलैंड) को भेजी, जिसका उन्हें स्वहस्तलिखित प्रत्युत्तर भी मिला।

Word Meaning

Invocation	– निवेदन	Cement	– मजबूत बनाना
Intently	– सावधानीपूर्वक	Occurrence	– किसी घटना का घटित होना
Convention	– तरीका	Distressed	– परेशान
Gewgaws	– अल्प महत्ता वाली वस्तुएँ	Fidelity	– विश्वसनीयता
Treacherous	– धूर्त	Bowel	– शरीर का एक अंग
Oppressor	– तानाशाह	Stagnating	– रुका हुआ
Folly	– मूर्खता	Animosity	– शत्रुता
Dwarfed	– छोटा कर देना	Sensation	– उत्तेजना का कारण
Delight	– आनन्द	Sentiments	– भावनाएँ
Ignorant	– अल्पज्ञानी	Vice	– बुरी आदत
Normal	– सामान्य	Instructor	– निर्देश देने वाला
Dilapidated	– बुरी दशा में	Earnestness	– गम्भीरता एवं सच्चाई
Provision	– प्रबन्ध	Luxury	– विलासिता की वस्तुएँ
Debt	– ऋण	Illustrating	– उदाहरण देना
Produce	– उत्पन्न करना	Community	– समुदाय, समूह विशेष
Worthless	– व्यर्थ, मूल्यहीन	Foundation	– आधारशिला
Simulated	– नकल किया हुआ		

Important Questions

Questions based on the Plot of the Chapter

Q 1. What was the focus point of the Atlanta Exposition speech given by Booker T Washington?

अटलांटा प्रदर्शनी में बुकर द्वारा दिए गए भाषण का सारांश क्या था?

बुकर का अटलांटा प्रदर्शनी में भाषण देना – बुकर का अनुभवी व्यक्ति होना – सकारात्मक रूप से भाषण देना – मैत्रीपूर्ण संबंधों एवं समानता का महत्त्व समझाना – जीवन को बेहतर बनाने का संदेश देना – तर्कपूर्ण ढंग से अपनी बात रखना।

Ans. Booker delivered a speech at Atlanta Exposition where his focus was only on harmonious relationship between two races. Booker was very experienced person, who was aware of the importance and benefits of friendliness and equality so he tried to give this message to everyone in a humble tone.

He put his focus on overall development and applying efforts for this. He tried to convince everyone by his proper logical statements. The overall effect of his speech was very positive because everyone wanted a social stability and harmony for sake of better living and peacefulness. Booker wanted to bridge the gap between white and Negro races, so he always focused on giving harmonious message to society.

Wherever he delivered public speeches, he only mentioned the benefits of unity and peaceful co-existence. The same pattern he followed in his speech in Atlanta Exposition also and tried to convince the people for adopting a peaceful living with better mutual understanding. The effect of Booker's speech was very positive on the people.

Q 2. How did the Southern audience react to Booker's speech at the Atlanta Exposition?

अटलांटा प्रदर्शनी में बुकर द्वारा दिए गए भाषण पर दक्षिण के स्रोताओं की क्या प्रतिक्रिया थी?

बुकर का दोनों जातियों के समक्ष अपना भाषण देना – बुकर का समानता के सिद्धान्त पर बल देना – दक्षिणी श्रोताओं द्वारा बुकर का पूर्ण समर्थन करना – नीग्रो जाति के लोगों से जुड़े तथ्य प्रस्तुत करना – गोरे लोगों का विश्वास बढ़ जाना।

Ans. Booker delivered his speech in front of people of both races and his speech received a warm welcome from both races. Booker focused on the theme of equality which was much influential for his speech

Booker said that equality and friendliness is a key of progress. The Southern audience completely accepted Booker's view and they provided him a signal of harmony by their cheerful consent. Booker presented his facts related to Negro people by which the Southern audience became more friendly towards Negro people.

Booker was happy because bringing the situation of pacific was his primary goal. Booker wanted to bring affinity between two races and for it, he applied every possible effort.

He did not want to criticise any race in front of people of other races because he knew that nothing could be changed by following such critical comments. Booker tried to highlight the achievements and efforts of Negro people so that other people could understand the importance of them.

15

The Secret of Success in Public Speaking

Booker Received a Warm Welcome for his Address

Booker's speeches had a great effect on people and he gradually became famous. He was being praised in newspapers also. Mr Creelman, the correspondent of the New York world, wrote that a Negro man stood before a great audience and delivered a speech that marked the beginning of a new era, that always will be remembered in the history of the South.

Boston transcript described Booker's speech, delivered in 1897 at Robert Gould Shaw monument in Boston, as something that filled the crowd with zeal and made them emotionally charged. Chicago Times-Herald also gave an important column to a speech by Booker in which he mentioned the sacrifices made by the coloured and asked the whites to give the black the highest opportunity to live for their own country.

Booker Analyzed Himself

Booker did not believe that one should speak unless he has a message to deliver. The average audience wants fact and not general statements or preaching moral lessons. He always felt nervous in the beginning and it always took about 10 minutes for him to master the audience. He used to regret if he missed out anything important in his speech. He liked talking to businessmen as they catch the point very quickly. Next, he preferred to speak to the audience of both the races from the Southern region.

15

The Secret of Success in Public Speaking

बुकर के भाषण का भली-भाँति स्वागत हुआ

Booker (बुकर) के व्याख्यानों का लोगों पर गहरा प्रभाव पड़ता था और धीरे-धीरे उनकी ख्याति बढ़ने लगी। समाचार-पत्रों में भी उनकी तारीफ की गई। New Your World (न्यूयॉर्क वर्ल्ड) के संवाददाता Mr Creelman (श्रीमान क्रीलमैन) ने लिखा कि एक नीग्रो व्यक्ति भारी सभा के समक्ष खड़ा हुआ एवं उसने एक भाषण दिया, जिसने एक नए युग की बुनियाद रखी, जिसे South (दक्षिण) के इतिहास में सदा याद रखा जाएगा।

बोस्टन के समाचार-पत्र ने बुकर के भाषण की व्याख्या की जो बोस्टन के 1897 ई. में Robert Gould Shaw (रॉबर्ट गुल्ड शॉ) स्मारक में दिया गया था, जिसने जनता को नए उत्साह से भर दिया एवं सोचने पर मजबूर कर दिया। Chicago Time Herald (शिकागो टाइम्स हेराल्ड) ने भी बुकर के भाषण पर एक महत्त्वपूर्ण स्तंभ दिया जिसमें उन्होंने नीग्रो जाति के व्यक्तियों के बलिदानों की चर्चा की तथा गोरे व्यक्तियों को नीग्रो व्यक्तियों को अपने देशा के लिए जी सकने का एक उच्च अवसर देने को।

बुकर ने अपनी समीक्षा की

बुकर का यह नहीं मानना था कि किसी को तभी कुछ कहना चाहिए जब उसके पास देने हेतु कोई संदेश हो। आम जनता तथ्यपरक मुद्दों को सुनना चाहती है, सामान्य कथन या उपदेश नहीं। वह आरंभ में सदैव असहज महसूस किया करते थे और वे श्रोताओं पर अपनी पकड़ बनाने के लिए उन्हें हमेशा लगभग 10 मिनट लगते थे। यदि अपने भाषण में वे कोई महत्त्वपूर्ण बिंदु भूल जाते थे, तो वे उसके लिए खेद अवश्य प्रकट करते थे। उन्हें उद्योगपतियों से बात करना पसंद था, क्योंकि वे उनकी बातों को कम समय में विश्लेषित कर लेते थे। इसके अतिरिक्त वे दक्षिण क्षेत्र की दोनों जातियों के श्रोताओं से बात करना पसंद करते थे।

Booker was Free to Work Willingly

The whole executive force of Tuskegee was so organised that the daily work of the school was done like a clock. Booker was extremely satisfied with this thing and so he felt a kind of freedom. This enabled Booker to travel extensively as and when required.

बुकर इच्छानुसार कार्य कर सकने हेतु स्वतंत्र थे

Tuskegee (टस्कजी) का संपूर्ण प्रबंधन इतना संगठित था कि विद्यालय का प्रतिदिन का कार्य एक घड़ी की तरह पूरा किया जाता था। बुकर इस बात से अत्यधिक संतुष्ट रहते थे तथा उनको इसी वजह से एक प्रकार की स्वतंत्रता का अनुभव होता था। इससे वे अपनी इच्छा एवं आवश्यकतानुसार यात्रा करने हेतु भी स्वतंत्र थे।

Word Meaning

Immortal – अमर
Fiery – अत्यंत गर्म
Bewitch – आनंद देना
Nimbus – प्रकाश
Commercial – व्यावसायिक
Compensation – पुरस्कार
Elocution – भाषण
Baser – निम्न गुणवत्ता वाला
Ovation – तीव्र प्रसन्नता
Remnants – बचे हुए
Vivid – दृष्टिगोचर
Crank – उन्मादी
Expenditures – खर्चे
Vex – चिंतित
Prophecy – अनुमान
Clinched – बंद
Delirium – उत्तेजना
Tremulous – काँपता हुआ
Fierce – अत्यंत तीव्र
Thawing – पिघलना
Sermon – नैतिक मुद्दा
Responsiveness – प्रतिक्रिया
Gallant – साहसी
Extinction – समाप्त
Perpetuate – जीवित रखना
Pertain – संबंध बताना
Inevitable – जिसे टाला न जा सके
Imitation – नकल

Important Questions

Questions based on the Plot of the Chapter

Q 1. What special qualities should an orator possess for effective public speaking according to Booker?

बुकर के अनुसार प्रभावी ढंग से भाषण देने हेतु किसी व्यक्ति में क्या गुण होने चाहिए?

बुकर का भाषण देना – दर्शको को मंत्रमुग्ध करना – वक्ता एकाग्रचित्त रहना – नियोजित व्याख्यान देना – बुकर का प्रसिद्ध वक्ता का होना

Ans. Booker learned the art of public speaking by practice and experiences so he was aware of the importance of effectiveness of speech in order to make listeners spell bound. According to Booker one should feel completely relaxed and confident during one's addressings if one wants to get audience connected.

In addition to this, Booker accepts that a good orator should not address merely for speaking because a preplanned addressing never leaves real impact on audience.

A speaker should remain concentrated so that no important point could get skipped. Booker became a famous orator because he always focused on relevant points during his speeches. Booker always spoke whatever was important and he used to present his views in concine way.

He suggested that the art of effective speaking can be achieved by proper practice and patience. Booker expressed his own views regarding better public speaking and his views became popular in later days.

Q 2. Give a brief account of the speech Booker delivered in the city of Boston.

बोस्टन प्रांत में बुकर व्दारा दिए गए भाषण का संक्षेप में वर्णन करिए।

बुकर को बोस्टन प्रांत में एक सभा को संबोधित करने का अवसर मिलना – बोस्टन के सभागार में पहुँचना – समानता, देशभक्ति एवं समाज पर अत्यधिक धनात्मक भाषण देना

Ans. Booker received an invitation to address the public in Boston which was an exciting offer for him. He reached the venue which was overcrowded and this was a pleasant feeling for him. His speech was based on brotherhood of man which left a positive influence on the audience.

A number of people was present to hear Booker's speech along with their families. Booker tried to focus on the equality, patriotism and other positive aspects of human society so his addressing was warmly welcomed by the audience. Booker got a chance to address mass so he performed his act with extreme care. People wanted to listen Booker because they were Booker's fans. The views and ideas which were presented by Booker received wide acceptance and appraisal.

Booker emphasised the requirement of love, affinity and better terms among people which left a heavily positive influence on the public mindset.

Q 3. What was the explanation given by Booker to the newspaper editor in response to his criticism of law and customs?

बुकर ने अपने कानून एवं रिवाजों की आलोचनात्मक समीक्षा के लेख के लिए समाचार-पत्र के संपादकों को क्या उत्तर दिया?

शिकागो के संपादक द्वारा नकारात्मक प्रतिक्रिया मिलना – बुकर का आत्मविश्वासी होना – बुकर द्वारा संपादक को उत्तर देने का निर्णय लेना – बुकर द्वारा समय का प्रयोग करना – अखबार द्वारा अच्छी प्रतिक्रिया प्राप्त होना

Ans. Booker received a criticised response from an editor of Chicago for his address. The editor wanted an explanation of Booker's address. Booker decided to response the editor and he said that he had made a rule never to say before a Northern audience anything that he would not say before a Southern audience.

Booker was not a biased person and his confidence and frankness were his biggest strength. Booker believed in truth and that's why he never became perplexed about any issue. Booker wanted to put his efforts for the development so he never wasted his valuable time in politics of allegation.

Booker could give a solid response to the newspaper editor, but he did not do so because he believed in process of progression only. He wanted to let everyone know about him by his works, not by his false words. Booker never promoted criticism in any way.

Questions based on the Character-Sketch

Q 4. Give a brief character-sketch of Booker as a public speaker.

एक वक्ता के रूप में बुकर की चारित्रिक विशेषताओं का वर्णन करिए।

बुकर का प्रसिद्ध वक्ता होना – कला को अभ्यास एवं अनुभव से सीखना – बुकर का आत्मविश्वास से युक्त होना – अपने भाषणों के दौरान जनता के मन मस्तिष्क से सीधा संवाद करना – बुकर द्वारा अपने भाषणों के लिए पूर्व योजना न बनाना – अधिकांश अवसरों पर बिना तैयारी के भाषण देना।

Ans. Booker became famous as an effective orator and he learned the art of public speaking by practice and experiences. *On the basis of this chapter, we see following characteristics in his character.*

Confident Speaker Booker was a confident speaker because he established a relationship with minds of his listeners which was very important for proper delivery of his thoughts to his listeners.

Believer of on the Spot Speaking Booker did not believe in prelanned speeches and most of the times he delivered his speech without prior preparations. He thought that preplanned speeches never leave much impact on the audience.

Thus, we can say that Booker was a confident speaker, who believed in speaking without any preparation.

Expert in Judging the Mood of Audience Booker was an expert because he used to get the idea of mood of audience and delivered his speech according to the demand of audiences. This was the biggest reason of his being a popular orator.

16

Europe

Booker Got a New Companion

Booker was very busy in his school and his involvement in social works was increasing. Tuskegee school was growing towards progress. During this time, Booker got married to Miss Margaret James Murray in 1893.

She was a teacher and lady principal at Tuskegee and the couple shared a passionate interest in the success of the school. Margaret was an aware lady and was involved in several organisations and worked with local people in different capacities.

Children of Booker Started their Profession

Booker's oldest child daughter, Portia was a dressmaker and also showed a talent for instrumental music and became a teacher at Tuskegee. Junior Booker, his second child, had mastered the brick mason's trade and aspired to be an architect. The youngest son, Ernest Davidson wanted to be a doctor. Booker's work never allowed him to spend enough time with his big family and this was his greatest regret.

Booker Got a Chance of Trip to Europe

Seeing the busy schedule of Mr Booker, some of his friends in Boston thought that Booker was in need of a rest and change. He had never been to Europe before as he thought that it was a luxury for whites only. Booker's friends arranged a trip to Europe for him and his newly wed third wife.

16

Europe

बुकर की मुलाकात एक नए साथी से हुई

बुकर अपने विद्यालय में अत्यधिक व्यस्त रहा करते थे तथा सामाजिक कार्यों में उनकी भागीदारी बढ़ने लगी थी। टस्कजी विद्यालय उन्नति की ओर अग्रसर था। इसी दौरान बुकर का विवाह मिस मार्गरेट जेम्स मुरे से 1893 ई, में हो गया।

वह टस्कजी विद्यालय में शिक्षिका एवं प्रधानाध्यापिका थी और दोनों ने विद्यालय की सफलता में तीव्र रूचि दिखाई। मार्गरेट एक जागरूक महिला थीं तथा वे विभिन्न संस्थाओं से जुड़ी हुई थीं। स्थानीय व्यक्तियों के साथ उन्होंने विभिन्न क्षेत्रों में सुधार कार्य किए।

बुकर के बच्चों ने अपना कार्यक्षेत्र चुना

बुकर की सबसे बड़ी पुत्री पोर्शिया एक परिधान निर्माता थी तथा उसने संगीत में भी योग्यता दिखाई और टस्कजी में शिक्षिका बन गई। उनकी द्वितीय संतान, जूनियर बुकर ने ईंटें बनाने की कला में महारत हासिल कर ली तथा वास्तुशिल्पी बनने का निर्णय लिया। सबसे छोटे पुत्र अर्नेस्ट डेविडसन की इच्छा चिकित्सक बनने की थी। बुकर के कार्य ने कभी भी उन्हें उनके परिवार को पर्याप्त देने की इजाजत नहीं दी और इसका उन्हें सदैव अफसोस रहा करता था।

बुकर को यूरोप यात्रा का अवसर मिला

बुकर की व्यस्तताओं को देखते हुए बोस्टन प्रांत में रह रहे उनके कुछ मित्रों ने यह सोचा कि बुकर को आराम तथा बदलाव की जरूरत है। वे कभी यूरोप नहीं गए थे, क्योंकि उन्हें लगता था कि यूरोप मात्र गोरे व्यक्तियों के लिए सुविधाजनक स्थल है। बुकर के मित्रों ने उनके एवं उनकी नवविवाहित तीसरी पत्नी के लिए यूरोप की यात्रा का प्रबंध किया।

Word Meaning

Native	– मूल निवासी	Enterprise	– कार्य
Fondness	– पसंद करना	Executive	– कार्यकारी
Federation	– संघ	Expenses	– खर्चें
Regularly	– नियमित रूप से	Privilege	– सम्मान
Devotional	– आध्यात्मिक	Pleasure	– आनंद
Inspiring	– प्रेरणादायी	Surprise	– आश्चर्य
Unusually	– असामान्य रूप से	Responsible	– जिम्मेदार, उत्तरदायी
Believe	– विश्वास	Unexpected	– जिसकी उम्मीद न की गई हो
Steadily	– अनवरत	Ape	– नकल
Erect	– बनाना, बुनियाद रखना	Consented	– सहमत
Cathedral	– बड़ा गिरिजाघर	Ambassador	– राजनयिक
Satisfactory	– संतोषजनक	Reception	– स्वागत समारोह
Anticipation	– किसी घटना की आशा करना		

Important Questions

Questions based on the Plot of the Chapter

Q 1. Give a brief account of the children of Booker T Washington.

बुकर के बच्चों का संक्षेप में वर्णन करिए।

बुकर के परिवार में तीन बच्चों का होना – बच्चों का अत्यंत प्रिय होना – बडी पुत्री पोर्शिया का परिधान निर्माता होना – बुकर के दूसरे पुत्र (टेलियाफेरो) का ईंटे बनाने की कला मे निपुण होना – छोटे पुत्र का चिकित्सक बनना – बच्चो का बुकर से शिकायत न होना – तीनों बच्चों का स्वयं कार्यक्षेत्र चुनना।

Ans. Booker had three children in his family, who were very dear to him. Portia was the eldest daughter of Booker, who was a dressmaker. She had also an unusual ability in instrumental music which ultimately led her towards teaching. Booker Taliaferro was Booker's next eldest son, who was expert in brick masons trade. Because of his this expertise, he started his profession as an architect. Booker's youngest son was Ernest Davidson Washington, who wanted to become a physician. Booker's children were quite sincere and self-motivated and Booker was happy with them.

Children of Booker were very sensitive and careful in their approach towards life. Booker could not give them proper time because of his various responsibilities, but his children never made any complain for this. Booker always tried to give them appropriate suggestions so that they could get a proper guideline for their future. All the three children of Booker selected their professions according to their own choices and Booker was proud of them.

Q 2. What were the two thoughts that disturbed Booker when he was thinking about going on a Europe tour?

जब बुकर यूरोप की यात्रा पर जाने की सोच रहे थे तब कौन-सी दो बातें उनके लिऐ चिंता का कारण बनी हुई थीं?

यूरोप यात्रा की योजना अचानक बनना – बुकर के मस्तिष्क में विभिन्न प्रकार की शंकाएँ उठना – बुकर का घमंडी तथा दिखावे की और आकर्षित होना – बुकर का हमेशा सादा जीवन जीना – बुकर द्वारा समाज के प्रति गलत व्यवहार न करना

Ans. The plan of Europe visit was sudden, unexpected and not made by Booker, but he had to go because of his well wisher's requests. Booker had various doubts and worries in his mind like he was thinking about peoples, reactions after knowing about his Europe trip.

Booker thought that people were not aware of circumstances of Booker's trip, so they might think that he had become proud after large scale fame. Except this, Booker was worried because his inner conscience would not allowing him to spare the time from his work which was a worship for him.

Booker always believed in living simple and straight life so he could not easily prepare himself for going on any kind of vacation or trip. Booker became ready for going only because of excessive requests of his well wisher friends, Booker was an educationist and social reformer also so he never tried to put any wrong example in front of society and according to him, going for a trip was not beneficial

Q 3. What thing impressed Booker a lot in Holland? Discuss.

बुकर को हॉलैण्ड में किस बात ने सबसे ज्यादा प्रभावित किया?

↗ बुकर को हॉलैण्ड घूमने का अवसर मिलना – पुराने जमाने की नाव में सफर करना – बुकर का हॉलैण्ड के पशुधन एवं खेती के प्रभावी तरीकों से अत्यधिक प्रभावित होना – बुकर का 400 अच्छी नस्ल की गायों को एक साथ चरते देखना शिक्षा के लिए बुकर को अन्य स्थानों पर जाने का अवसर मिलना

Ans. Booker got a chance to visit Holland during his trip which was a positive experience for him. He got the chance of sailing in old fashioned canal boats which was quite different experience for him. Booker was heavily impressed by the thoroughness of the agriculture and the excellence of the holstein cattle in Holland. Before visiting Holland, he could never imagine about such effective utilisation of land anywhere. He observed there almost 400 fine breed holstein cows grazing in one of intensely green fields. This really amazed Booker very much.

Booker got various chances of going and visiting various places in order to expand his mission of education, but when he visited Holland, he became very surprised. He found there various specialities which made him stunned. Booker observed the people of Holland using animal resources in most effective way. He understood the agricultural pattern of Holland and became very satisfied because they were involved in agriculture using much progressed means of agriculture.

Q 4. What was Booker's conviction which got further reinforced by his meeting the famous American Negro painter, Mr Henry Tanner?

प्रख्यात अमेरिकन नीग्रो चित्रकार हेनरी टेनर से मुलाकात के बाद बुकर की कौन-सी विचारधारा और मजबूत हो गई?

↗ बुकर को विख्यात अमेरिकी नीग्रो चित्रकार हेनरी टेनर से मिलने का अवसर प्राप्त होना – कला एवं चित्रकारी के गुणों के कारण पेरिस में प्रख्यात होना – बुकर की सोच का दृढ़ होना – बुकर का हेनरी टेनर से मिलना – हेनरी टेनर का नीग्रो जाति से सम्बन्ध होना।

Ans. Booker got a chance to meet with a famous American Negro painter Henry Tanner, which gave him a pleasant surprise. Henry Tanner was a Negro but he became very famous in Paris because of his command over art and painting.

People of Paris believed in his abilities after seeing his work. Booker meeting with Henry made his faith more firm that any man, regardless of colour would be recognised and rewarded if he learns to do something in a well manner. Booker was free from racial bonds so he never underestimated any person's potential and it is true that talent is never useless for anyone.

Booker always believed that presence of any kind of expertise results in reward. Booker was true because when he met with Henry Tanner he became surprised by seeing his quality paintings. He came to know that he was very famous in America because of his painting speciality.

Henry belonged to the Negro race, but people could not ignore him. This was a very satisfying thing for Booker and he began to feel proud of that Negro painter.

Questions based on the Character-sketch

Q 5. Give a brief character-sketch of Booker?

बुकर की चारित्रिक विशेषताओं का वर्णन करिए।

बुकर का किसी प्रकार की यात्रा में दिलचस्पी न होना – मित्रों का उनके लिए यात्रा का प्रबंध करना – बुकर का अपने सामाजिक सरोकारों के प्रति समर्पित होना – बुकर का अपने कर्त्तव्यों के प्रति पूर्णरूप से समर्पित होना – अपनी यात्रा के दौरान उन्हें हर जगह भरपूर स्वागत एवं समर्थन मिलना।

Ans. Booker was not interested in any trip. His friends arranged a trip for him and convinced him to go for the trip. Booker was dedicated towards his social concerns. *On the basis of this chapter, we see following traits in his character*

Dedicated Towards his Duties Booker was much dedicated towards his duties because when he was given a chance of trip arranged by his friends, he could not prepare himself for this. It was useless to wander here and there according to him.

Famous Person Booker was a very famous person because during his trip, he received a warm welcome everywhere. He was a well known face because of his philanthropic deeds.

Thus, we can say that Booker was a famous person who was dedicated towards his duties also.

17

Last Words

General Armstrong's Visited Tuskegee Last Time

Six months before he died, General Armstrong expressed a wish to visit Tuskegee. His wish was fulfilled and he was brought to Tuskegee school by a special train, arranged by the whites free of cost.

He spent two months in Booker's home. Even in paralised state, he never stopped thinking about how to help the South overcome the slavery. At the last moment of his life again he told Booker that it was not only the duty of the country to uplift not only the Negroes of the South but also the poor white people. He died a short time later.

Booker Bagged Another Rarest Achievement

Booker T Washington got the greatest surprise and the highest point of his lifetime, when he became the first to receive an honorary degree from the prestigious Harvard University. During the conferring of the degree, excitement and enthusiasm were at the highest pitch. In his speech at Harvard, Booker stressed the need to uplift the poorest, most ignorant and humblest.

President McKinley Praised Booker

Booker met the American President and requested him to pay a visit to his school as a great encouragement for his teachers and the students. The President made a visit to the school on 16th December. All the achievements of the school were paraded. The President McKinley appreciated Booker's efforts in helping the students to lead a life of dignity and honour by being self-reliant. Booker's school was considered a 'spectacle'.

17

Last Words

जनरल आर्मस्ट्राँग ने अंतिम बार टस्कजी का दौरा किया

अपनी मृत्यु से छह: महीने पूर्व General Armstrong (जनरल आर्मस्ट्राँग) ने एक बार टस्कजी की यात्रा करने की इच्छा व्यक्त की। उनकी इच्छा को पूरा किया गया और गोरे व्यक्तियों ने एक विशिष्ट रेलगाड़ी द्वारा उन्हें निशुल्क Tuskegel (टस्कजी) विद्यालय पहुँचाया।

उन्होंने बुकर के घर में दो माह का समय बिताया। अपहिजता की स्थिीत में भी उन्होंने यह सोचना नहीं छोड़ा कि दक्षिण को दासता से मुक्ति दिलाने हेतु किस प्रकार सहायता की जाए। उन्होंने अपने जीवन के अंतिम क्षणों के दौरान बुकर को बताया कि देश की जिम्मेदारी है कि वह न केवल दक्षिण के Negroes (नीग्रो) अपितु गरीब गोरे व्यक्तियों का भी उत्थाने करे। कुछ समय बाद ही उनका निधन हो गया।

बुकर ने एक और दुर्लभ उपलब्धि हासिल की

Booker T Washington (बुकर टी वाशिंगटन) के लिए सर्वाधिक आश्चर्य एवं जीवन का प्रसन्न्तम क्षण तब आया जब वे पतिष्ठित Harvard University (हावर्ड विश्वविद्यालय) की तरफ से एक सम्माननीय उपाधि पाने वाले पहले नीग्रो बने। उपाधि वितरण समारोह के दौरान उलजना तथा उत्साह अपने उच्चतम बिंदु पर थे हावर्ड में अपने अपने भाषण में बुकर ने गरीब, पिछड़ें एवं निम्न वर्ग के व्यक्तियों के उत्थान की जरूरतों पर जोर दिया।

राष्ट्रपति मैकिनले ने बुकर की प्रशंसा की

बुकर American President (अमेरिकी राष्ट्रपति) से मिले तथा उनसे अपने छात्रों एवं अध्यापकों के उत्साहवर्द्धन हेतु विद्यालय की यात्रा का निवेदन किया। राष्ट्रपति महोदय 16 दिसंबर को विद्यालय का भ्रमण करने पहुँचे। विद्यालय की सभी उपलब्धियों की चर्चा की गई। विद्यार्थियों को आत्मविश्वास के साथ एक सम्मानपूर्ण जीवन जीने के योग्य बनाने में सहायता करने हेतु President Mckinley (राष्ट्रपति मैकिनले) ने बुकर की प्रशंसा की। बुकर का विद्यालय एक आदर्श उदाहरण बन गया था।

Glory of Tuskegee School

The school owned 2,300 acres of land, 66 buildings all except 4 totally built by the students. There were 30 industrial departments in the school. There was proper arrangement for academic and spiritual learning. There were 1400 students which initially were 30 in number.

The girls also got training in gardening, fruit growing, dairying, bee-culture and poultry raising. Booker organised annual gatherings for ex-students, many more gatherings and conferences to make the school best in the world.

टस्कजी विद्यालय का बढ़ता हुआ गौरव

विद्यालय लगभग 2,300 एकड़ भूमि में था, जिसमें 66 इमारतें थीं, जिनमें से 4 के अतिरिक्त सभी विद्यार्थियों द्वारा बनाई गई थीं। विद्यालय में 30 औद्योगिक विभाग थे। अध्ययन एवं आध्यात्म दोनों के प्रशिक्षण की अति उत्तम व्यवस्था थी। छात्रों की संख्या 1400 थी जो प्रारंभ में 30 थी।

छात्राओं को भी बागवानी, फल उगाना, दुग्ध उद्योग, मधुमक्खी पालन तथा मुर्गीपालन औद्योगिक बुकर ने पूर्व छात्रों के लिए सम्मेलन भी आयोजित किए, बहुत से सम्मेलन विद्यालय को विश्व का सर्वोत्तम बनाने के लिए थे।

Word Meaning

Gratified – उपकृत
Anew – पुन: प्रारंभ करना
Hesitation – संकोच
Prominence – महत्ता
Inventor – प्रारंभकर्ता
Alumni – पूर्व छात्रों का समूह
Crucible – कठिन परीक्षा
Condoling – सहानुभूति जताना
Opinion – विचार
Intimate – सूचना देना
Auspices – सहयोग
Exalt – स्तर ऊँचा उठाना
Vocations – कार्य
Mortgage – ऋण
Novel – नवीन
Acquainted – परिचित
Ostracism – सामाजिक बहिष्करण
Wealth – धन
Popularity – लोकप्रियता
Inappropriate – गलत
Patriot – देशभक्त
Honorary – सम्मान
Vicinity – आसपास का क्षेत्र
Adjourn – बर्खास्त
Conception – विचारधारा
Conservative – रूढ़िवादी
Domestic – घरेलू
Institution – संस्था

Important Questions

Questions based on the Plot of the Chapter

Q 1. Why did General Armstrong make a visit to Tuskegee even in paralysed state? How was the welcome given to him by the school and the community?

गंभीर रूप से बीमार होने की दशा में भी जनरल, आर्मस्ट्राँग ने टस्कजी का दौरा क्यों किया? विद्यालय एवं समुदाय के लोगों ने उनका स्वागत कैसे किया?

जनरल आर्मस्ट्राँग का एक जिम्मेदार व्यक्ति होना – समान अवसरों के लिए पक्षधर होना – बीमारी की दशा में टस्कजी का दौरा करना – उनके सम्मान में एक विशेष रेलगाड़ी का प्रबंध होना – जनरल आर्मस्ट्राँग का टस्कजी पहुँचना

Ans. General Armstrong was a responsible person, who was in favour of equal growth opportunity for everyone. He was at the last stage of life, so he wanted to give some advices and suggestions regarding upliftment of public to his dearest pupil Booker, so he decided to visit Tuskegee even in paralysed state. A special arrangement of train was done for him and he reached Tuskegee. When he reached Tuskegee, thousand students, teachers and other people welcomed him with a great enthusiasm which made General Armstrong overwhelmed.

He met with Booker and reminded him about various responsibilities. General Armstrong lived his life in an inspiring way and he left an ideal example to be followed. He always focused on the importance of education and tried to expand positive messages in society. People respected him very much and Booker also respected him as his real mentor. General Armstrong wanted to give his last lesson to his dearest student Booker, so he decided to visit Tuskegee and meet with Booker as well as students of the institute.

Q 2. What was Booker's reaction to the news of his getting honorary degree from Harvard University?

हार्वर्ड विश्वविद्यालय व्दारा सम्माननीय उपाधि मिलने की सूचना पर बुकर की क्या प्रतिक्रिया थी?

बुकर का अपने विभिन्न गुणों के कारण प्रसिद्ध होना – हार्वर्ड विश्वविद्यालय द्वारा एक सम्माननीय उपाधि मिलना – खुशी के आँसू आना – विख्यात विश्वविद्यालय से उपाधि मिलना – बुकर की जिंदगी मे उतार-चढ़ाव आना – बुकर का साहस बनाए रखना।

Ans. Booker became very famous because of his various qualities, so he received a letter in which he got an invitation from Harvard University for being offered an honorary degree. This incident made him almost speechless and fully overwhelmed. After reading the letter, his eyes were filled with tears.

He recalled earlier moments of his life including all ups and downs like his slavery days, his struggle for earnings, his struggle for his education, his adverse conditions, his struggle for Tuskegee School project and rest of everything. It was the greatest honour for him to receive a degree from a reputed university. He was quite contented after getting this news. Booker's life was full of ups and downs because of his uncertain and depressive circumstances, but he never surrendered and continued his efforts for making things improved.

Q 3. What were paper's views about conferring honorary degree of Mr Washington at Harvard?

हार्वर्ड विश्वविद्यालय व्दारा बुकर को उपाधि दिए जाने पर समाचार-पत्रों ने क्या प्रतिक्रिया दी?

बुकर के उपाधि ग्रहण के समाचार पत्रों को अत्यधिक प्रचारित करना – न्यूयॉर्क के अखबार में बुकर के सम्मान को प्रेरणादायक तरीके से प्रस्तुत करना – विश्वविद्यालय द्वारा सम्मान देने के निर्णय को उचित बताना – न्यूयॉर्क टाइम्स में बुकर की उपाधि का वर्णन होना – प्रत्येक अखबार में बुकर का वर्णन होना – बुकर की सफलता को बड़े स्तर पर प्रदर्शित करना।

Ans. The event of receiving degree of Booker was appreciated in newspapers. Every newspaper presented a positive comment on this news. A New York paper wrote that Booker received his degree with a great honour in presence of an enthusiastic crowd. This paper also presented this news in positive and inspiring way. Similarly, a Boston paper appreciated Booker for his education, responsible citizenship and efforts of upliftment of people of every race and justified the decision of university administration of honouring Booker.

A newspaper named New York Times also praised Booker for his abilities and justified his worthiness. Conclusively, it can be said that print-media welcomed Booker. The event of reception of Booker became a most appreciated and covered incident by media. Almost every newspaper admired Booker for his this achievement. Booker belonged to Negro race, but inspite of having various drawbacks in his life, he always led an inspiring life. When his efforts got noticed at large scale, media began to praise him for his efforts made for the development of society and his race.

Questions based on the Character-Sketch

Q 4. Draw the character-sketch of President McKinley of the US.

अमेरिका के राष्ट्रपति मैकिनले का चरित्र चित्रण करिए।

मैकिनले, अमेरिका के राष्ट्रपति का व्यस्त इंसान होना – राष्ट्रपति का अत्यंत विनम्र होना – मैकिनले का संभ्रांत व्यक्ति का होना – सम्पूर्ण जिम्मेदारियाँ उठाना

Ans. McKinley was the President of United States, who was a busy person. Being an important person, he was much respected, but he was very humble.

On the basis of this chapter, we see following traits in his character

A Well Mannered Person President McKinley was a well mannered person because inspite of having various responsibilities at same time, he never lost his temper. He always behave in a balanced way which was not an easy task in those adverse conditions.

Down to Earth Person President McKinley was a down to Earth person also because when Booker requested him to visit his school for encouragement of his staff and students, he became ready to do so without making any excuse.

Thus, it can be said that Mr McKinley was a well mannered person, who was down to Earth also.

QUESTION DIGEST

Q 1. What do you know about Booker's early childhood, family and home?

बुकर के प्रारंभिक जीवन, पारिवारिक पृष्ठभूमि एवं परिवार के विषय में आप क्या जानते हैं?

Ans. As a slave child, living on a plantation, Booker lived with his mother Jane, his brother John and sister Amanda. They lived in cabin that also served as the plantation's kitchen. His mother was the plantation cook. The early years of his life which were spent in the little cabin were not different from those of thousands of other slaves. His mother had little time for her children. She stole a few moments for their care in the early morning the daily activities.

Booker recollects his mother cooking a chicken late at night and awakening her children for the purpose of feeding them. He did not know how or where she got it from. He did not remember having slept on a bad until after their family was declared free. The three children had a mattress of straw on the dirt floor or they slept on a bundle of filthy rags laid upon the dirt.

He knew almost nothing of his ancestry. His mother had a step sister and a step brother. He knew even less of his father than what he knew of his mother. He did not even know the name of his father. He had heard that his father was a white man who lived in a nearby plantation. His father had never taken interest in Booker or contributed in any way to his upbringing.

Q 2. While at Hampton, what did Booker learn, besides book knowledge?

हैंपटन में बुकर ने किताबी ज्ञान के अतिरिक्त और क्या-क्या सीखा?

Ans. The education that Booker received at Hampton out of the text books was just a small part of what he learnt there. One of things that deeply impressed him learning the second year was the unselfishness of the teachers. It was very difficult for him to understand how individuals could bring themselves to the point where they could be very happy in working for others.

Before the end of the year, he began to learn that those persons were the happiest who did the most for others. Booker tried to carry this lesson with him throughout. He also learnt a valuable lesson at Hampton by corning into contact with the best breeds of livestock and fowls.

According to him, no student, who had the opportunity of doing this could go out into the world and content himself with the poorest grades. He also started understanding the use and value of the Bible, not only for spiritual help, but also in account of its as literature. Booker made it a rule to read a chapter or a portion of a chapter in the morning, before beginning his work of the day. Such was the impact of the learning he got at Hampton.

Q 3. What gave Booker the rest and enjoyment?

बुकर को किस बात से विश्राम और आनंद मिलता था?

Ans. The time when Booker got the rest and recreation was when he could be at Tuskegee and after the evening meal, could sit down, Booker,Davidson and their three children read a story and each took turns in telling a story.

For Booker, there was nothing equal to that and he would go out on Sunday afternoons into the woods to enjoy the bounties of nature where no one could disturb him. He would be surrounded by pure air, the trees, the shrubbery, the flowers and the fragrance of flowers and would be able to enjoy the chirping of crickets and songs of the birds.

Booker's garden was another source of rest and enjoyment. He liked to touch nature, the real thing. When he could leave his office in time, he would love to spend sometime in spading the ground, planting seeds and digging about the plants. He could derive great strength from all that.

He derived a great deal of pleasure in raising pigs and fowls. Booker did not care for games. He had never seen a game of football. Few things were more satisfaction to him than a high grade Berkshire on Poland China Pig.

Q 4. What lessons did Booker T. Washington learn from General Armstrong?

बुकर टी वाशिंगटन ने जनरल आर्मस्ट्रांग से क्या सीखा?

Ans. The first visit which General Armstrong made to Tuskegee gave Booker an opportunity to get an insight into his character deeply. Booker very soon learned that General Armstrong was as anxious about the prosperity and the happiness of the white race as the black. He cherished no bitterness against the South and was happy when an opportunity was offered for manifesting his sympathy.

Booker had never heard Armstrong speaking, in public or in private a single bitter word against the white men in the South. Hence, he learned the lesson that assistance given to the weak makes one who gives it strong and that subjection of the unfortunate makes one weak. Hence, he decided never to hate anyone, irrespective of the colour. The credit for the efforts put for securing industrial education for white boys and girls goes to General Armstrong.

The gospel of the toothbrush as General Armstrong used to call it was a part of creed at Tuskegee. No student, who did not keep and use a toothbrush was permitted to retain. General Armstrong was for above the ordinary individual.

When Booker was in the midst of great anxiety, regarding funds for the new building, he received a telegram from Armstrong asking him to spend a month travelling with him through the North.

They hold meetings in which Booker was to speak. The General was too big to be little, too good to be mean. He knew that the people in the North, who gave money, gave it for the purpose of helping the whole cause of Negro civilisation and not for one school. In regard to the addresses which Booker had to make in the North, he recalled just one piece of advice that the General gave him, that was, "give them an idea for every word."

Before Six months of his death, General Armstrong expressed a wish to visit Tuskegee. He remained as a guest at Booker's home for about two months and without the use of voice or limb, he spent every hour in devising ways and means to help the South. He insisted that it was not the duty of the country to assist the Negro in elevating. General Armstrong gave Booker the privilege of getting acquainted with his successor, Dr Frissell who hid his own personality behind that of General Armstrong.

Character Sketchs

Booker T. Washington

This man's magic shines throughout his autobiography. In fact, he was very modest about his accomplishments. His life was amazing, because he took himself out of slavery and was full of determination to pull his people up with him. He took every opportunity to propose his ideas and philosophies to all races so that attitudes could change in America. He saw that many terrible things were happening to his people, but still he remained quite optimistic that, with the help of education and hard work, they could effectively integrate with the dominant white society. He became famous because of his good works but never sought it out. He devoted his life to his students as well as his race and was sure that the day was not far when the black man would be totally accepted throughout the country.

Booker's Mother

Booker's mother had a great influence on Booker's life. She had lived nearly all of her life as a slave but was never a pessimist. She never gave up hope that the Emancipation would come. She was a great supporter of Booker in every venture he tried, especially that of his extreme desire for education. She very well understood how much the wearing of a cap to school meant to Booker and in spite of her extreme poverty she found a way to make one for him. Booker said that never ever any cap or hat meant as much to him. She taught him the lesson of self-respect and dignity of labour.

Mrs. Ruffner

Mrs. Ruffner was the wife of owner of the salt mine where Booker worked in Maiden, West Virginia. She was a strict boss and many had quit the job or had been fired. Booker learnt that to make her happy, one had to understand that she wanted things clean, done promptly and systematically and wanted honesty and frankness.

चरित्र चित्रण

बुकर टी. वाशिंगटन

उपन्यास का सर्वाधिक प्रधान चरित्र जिसका महत्त्व संपूर्ण उपन्यास में परिलक्षित होता है। Booker T Washington (बुकर टी. वाशिंगटन) एक महान् व्यक्ति थे, जो अपनी महान उपलब्धियों के बावजूद अत्यंत विनम्र थे। उनका जीवन आश्चर्यों से भरा हुआ था, क्योंकि उन्होंने स्वयं को दासता के अँधेरे से मुक्त कराया तथा अपनी जाति के लोगों की भलाई हेतु कार्य किया। उन्होंने America (अमेरिका) में सभी जाति के लोगों को अपने विचार समझाए एवं लोगों के नजरिये को बदलने का प्रयास किया। उन्होंने देखा कि उनकी जाति के लोगों के साथ बहुत बुरा बर्ताव हो रहा था, परंतु वे आशावादी थे एवं उन्होंने उम्मीद जारी रखी कि परिश्रम एवं शिक्षा के बल पर उनकी जाति के लोग भी श्वेत समुदाय की बराबरी करने में सफल होंगे। वे अपने महान् कार्यों की वजह से विख्यात हो गए। उन्होंने अपना संपूर्ण जीवन अपने विद्यार्थियों के हित में तथा अपनी जाति के उत्थान में अर्पित कर दिया, क्योंकि उन्हें पूर्ण विश्वास था कि एक दिन ऐसा अवश्य आएगा जब Negro (नीग्रो) जाति के लोग पूर्ण विश्व में स्वीकार किए जाएँगे।

बुकर की माता

बुकर की माता एक महान् महिला थीं तथा बुकर के जीवन पर उनकी गहन छाप पड़ी थी। बुकर की माता ने अपना पूरा जीवन एक दास के रूप में व्यतीत किया, परंतु वे कभी निराशावादी नहीं रहीं। उन्होंने आजादी का दामन थामे रखा तथा उसकी अपेक्षा जारी रखी। उन्होंने बुकर का साथ उनके जीवन के हर कार्य में दिया, विशेषकर शिक्षा प्राप्ति की लालसा में। वे अच्छी तरह समझती थीं कि बुकर के लिए विद्यालय के क्या मायने हैं अत: वे अपनी आर्थिक दुश्वारियों के बावजूद बुकर को संसाधन उपलब्ध कराने हेतु प्रतिबद्ध एवं प्रयासरत रहीं। बुकर की माता ने उनके लिए एक टोपी का इंतजाम किया, जिसे बुकर ने सदा बहुमूल्य माना। बुकर की माता ने बुकर को परिश्रम तथा आत्मसम्मान की महत्ता का पाठ पढ़ाया।

श्रीमती रफनर

Mrs Ruffner (श्रीमती रफनर) उस नमक की खान के स्वामी की पत्नी थीं, जिस खान में बुकर ने कार्य किया था एवं जो West Virginia (दक्षिण वर्जीनिया) में स्थित थी। वे एक कड़क मिजाज स्वामिनी थीं तथा इस कारण से उनके लिए काम करने वाले नौकरों को काम छोड़ देना पड़ता था अथवा वे उन्हें पदच्युत कर दिया करती थीं। बुकर ने यह अनुभव किया कि श्रीमती रफनर को प्रसन्न करने हेतु यह समझना आवश्यक था कि वे कार्यों को पूर्ण स्वच्छता के साथ, शीघ्रतापूर्वक तथा व्यवस्थित ढंग से किया जाना पसंद करती थीं

They developed a great friendship based on trust. She became a valuable friend who taught him a great deal about cleanliness and the dignity of work when he had taken a position in her home.

General Samuel C. Armstrong

General Armstrong was the person Booker admired the most in the world. After the Civil War, he took it upon himself to find a way to educate the black people and help them integrate with the dominant white society. As a result, he established the Hampton Institute and that is where Booker attended school. He was the one who made the greatest impression on Booker, who considered him to be one of the noblest and rarest of human beings. He was unselfish and was worshipped by his students. General Armstrong's philosophies about how education and work go hand-in-hand later influenced Booker into applying them to his own educational ideas. He was too big to be little, too good to be mean. He knew that the way to strengthen Hampton was to make it a centre of unselfish power.

Miss Mary F. Mackie

Miss Mary F. Mackie was the first person whom Booker met when he arrived at Hampton. On reaching there he was awestruck by the beauty of the school building and believed his life to have a new meaning. He could not make a favourable impression on the head teacher, Miss Mackie, since he was shabbily dressed. He had to change her opinion so when she sent him into an adjoining room and asked him to sweep it, he realised she was a yankee woman. She thought he needed a test to prove he was, worthy of acceptance. Though hard, he stuck to the work. Later, Miss Mackie became one of his strongest and helpful friends. She taught him the dignity of labour. Miss Nathalie Lord: One teacher, Miss Nathalie Lord, taught Booker the use and value of the Bible. He learnt that the happiest are those who do the most for others. She even made Booker aware that he needed to be able to speak to the world if he were going to help it. Miss Lord found out that Booker had some inclination towards public speaking, so she gave him private lessons in the matter of breathing, emphasis and articulation.

इसके अतिरिक्त वे ईमानदारी एवं निष्कपटता को पसंद करती थीं। शीघ्र ही बुकर एवं रफनर के मध्य विश्वास की नींव पर एक बेहतर रिश्ता कायम हो गया। श्रीमती रफनर बुकर की विश्वसनीय मित्र हो गईं तथा उन्होंने बुकर को सफाई, आत्मसम्मान एवं अन्य सद्गुणों के महत्त्व के विषय में बताया।

जनरल सैमुअल सी. आर्मस्ट्रांग

जनरल आर्मस्ट्रांग ऐसे व्यक्ति थे, जिनकी बुकर ने सर्वाधिक प्रशंसा की। युद्ध के पश्चात् जनरल आर्मस्ट्रांग ने स्वयं के प्रयासों से नीग्रो जाति को शिक्षित करने का जिम्मा लिया, जिससे वे भी प्रभावशाली श्वेत समुदाय के समान हो सकें। इस कारण उन्होंने हैंपटन इंस्टीट्यूट की स्थापना की तथा वही वह संस्थान था, जहाँ बुकर का अध्ययन हुआ तथा उन्हें शिक्षित होकर देश के लिए कुछ करने का अवसर मिला। जनरल आर्मस्ट्रांग उन व्यक्तियों में से थे, जिन्होंने बुकर पर गहन छाप छोड़ी थी तथा बुकर भी जनरल आर्मस्ट्रांग को सज्जनतम पुरुष मानते थे तथा सम्मान देते थे। जनरल आर्मस्ट्रांग स्वार्थहीन व्यक्ति थे तथा उनके शिष्य उनकी पूजा करते थे। जनरल आर्मस्ट्रांग के विचार कि ''किस प्रकार शिक्षा एवं व्यावहारिक कौशल साथ-साथ सीखे जाएँ'' ने बुकर को भी प्रभावित किया एवं बाद में उन्होंने भी शिक्षक रहते हुए यही पद्धति अपनाई। वे अत्यंत उदार हृदय थे, वे अत्यंत सच्चे थे। वे मानते थे कि हैंपटन को सुदृढ़ बनाने हेतु इसे स्वार्थहीन शक्ति का केन्द्र बनाना आवश्यक था।

मैरी एफ. मैकी

मैरी एफ. मैकी प्रथम महिला थीं, जिनसे बुकर हैंपटन पहुँचने के पश्चात् सर्वप्रथम मिले। हैंपटन पहुँचने के पश्चात् उनकी आँखें आश्चर्य से विस्मित हो गईं, जब उन्होंने वहाँ विद्यालय का भवन देखा तथा उन्हें प्रशंसापूर्वक भवन को देखते रहने की इच्छा हुई, इस अनुभव ने उनकी जिंदगी को एक नया उद्देश्य दिया। वे मैरी एफ. मैकी पर अच्छा प्रभाव नहीं छोड़ सके, क्योंकि उन्होंने अत्यंत गंदे वस्त्र पहन रखे थे। बुकर मैरी को प्रभावित करना चाहते थे अत: जब वे कमरे में गए, तथा मैरी एफ. मैकी ने उन्हें कमरे की सफाई करने को कहा, तो उन्होंने हामी भर दी। मैरी एफ. मैकी चाहती थीं कि बुकर यह सिद्ध करें कि वे इस योग्य हैं कि उन्हें प्रवेश दिया जाए। वे अपने उद्देश्य में सफल रहे तथा बाद के दिनों में मैरी एफ. मैकी बुकर के अच्छे दोस्तों में से एक हो गईं। उन्होंने बुकर को श्रम की महत्ता का पाठ पढ़ाया। नताली लॉर्ड, जो एक अध्यापिका थीं, ने भी बुकर को सद्गुणों की सीख दी तथा पवित्र धर्मग्रंथ बाइबिल का अनुसरण करने की सीख दी। बुकर ने सीखा कि सबसे प्रसन्न वे लोग होते हैं, जो दूसरों के लिए भलाई के कार्य करते हैं। बुकर जानते थे कि लोगों की मदद करने हेतु लोगों से संवाद करना अत्यंत आवश्यक होगा अत: वे इस दिशा में प्रयत्नशील हो गए। श्रीमती लॉर्ड ने अनुभव किया कि बुकर जन संवाद की प्रक्रिया में सहज नहीं थे अत: उन्होंने बुकर की यथासंभव मदद की तथा उन्हें कुशल वक्ता बनने हेतु प्रेरित किया।

www.ingramcontent.com/pod-product-compliance
Ingram Content Group UK Ltd.
Pitfield, Milton Keynes, MK11 3LW, UK
UKHW021656190726
13853UKWH00001B/292

9 789351 765288